The Cost of Standing while Staying

The Sequel to My Safe Haven

YAVON SMITH

All scriptural quotations are from the *King James Version of the Holy Bible*

The Cost of Standing while Staying

Published by: Yavon Smith

Book Production by: Yavon Smith

Printed in the United States of America

Table of Contents

Dedication

This book is dedicated to those who are struggling with their identity in Christ Jesus. It is also for those who continue to fight the good fight of faith, even if it seems as if you're the only one fighting. I pray this book will bless some who are walking with God while fighting to keep themselves and their family together.

I wrote this hoping that it will also bless wives who are just learning how to stand in the gap for their husbands, children, and themselves. I didn't forget the husbands either. I pray that you understand the enemy not only comes after you as the head, but he also comes after your wife, who is your helpmate. It takes a brave person to stand up for what God puts together.

At some point, the husband and wife will have to ask themselves, which one of us, if not both of us, is going to stand and fight?!

So, I am dedicating this book to you, my brother or sister. May God continue to strengthen and build you up to stand against the wiles of the devil, in Jesus' name!!

Your sister in Christ,

Nikki

Introduction

Hello, my brother or sister!!! Welcome back! I take it that you all have finished reading my first book. First of all, I want to thank you for your support and for reading the first part of my testimony. If you haven't, please, feel free to check out my book, titled; "My Safe Haven," and for those who have read it from start to end, I pray that it has helped you in several ways and that you are at a better place in your walk with the Lord because of it.

I thank my Heavenly Father for giving me another opportunity to write the second half of my testimony. As I walked through those chapters of my life, I needed to understand that God was not surprised by any of it! So, I say to you, nothing you have cried through, hurt through, done to yourself or others is a surprise to Him. Before I begin the second half of my testimony, I hope that reading this book will give you some insight into the next phase of my walk with God. During this process, I began to see things changing in the different seasons of my journey, which prompted me to write my first book. I felt compelled to take another look into the direction I was headed.

Trust me, my brother or sister, the things I experienced were nothing I would have *planned* for myself. If it had been left up to me, things would not have turned out the way they have. Consequently, there will have to be some transparency in this book, not to hurt anyone's feelings; however, without it, you wouldn't be able to fully understand what it cost me to "***stand while staying***."

I realized that something was happening in me; God was changing my thought processes.

"Therefore, if any man be in Christ, he is a new creature: old things are passed away; behold, all things are become new." **2 Corinthians 5:17, KJV**

I guess every once in a while, believers walk around, living life as if God isn't doing anything special in us. We are so focused on being blessed or looking for a blessing that we begin to take Him for granted. Well, the time may come when you are pushed back into a corner with nowhere to turn to. You will eventually try to come out by kicking, screaming, and fighting back, and that's when your eyes will open. You will start to see how the enemy blindsided you and was hiding ***(but working)*** all this time, but you never recognized him.

When you are actively trying to do the Will of God, the enemy knows God will shake things up in your life because of His Purpose and Plans for you. Satan will come at you more boldly; he will try to distract and make you want to give up, especially when you are unaware of his tricks. But you know what I figured out? Just as Satan attacked Job to curse God, I also felt that I was a target the enemy had focused on. He tried his best to make me give up on God, but the point I want to make is that God ***ALREADY KNEW*** what the outcome would be! I just had to stand!

One of the reasons I believe God allowed these things to take place in my life is because He knew I was that girl who would not back down without a fight! Have you ever been tired of being picked on? I was bullied every other day at school and on several different occasions during my childhood. You get tired of people messing with you, so you start fighting back, and you don't care who gets hurt; you go into defense mode, so you don't get hurt. Well, as an adult, a church girl or boy, as a woman of God or man of God, a person trying to live according to the Bible, a child of God, whatever you want to call yourself, we can allow our flesh to get in the *way* of not letting God handle the things we are faced with.

"And all this assembly shall know that The LORD saveth not with sword and spear: for the battle is The LORD's and He will give you into our hands." **1 Samuel 17:47, KJV**

I think it's pretty safe to say that we have all had moments where we didn't quite take our hand out of the battle. It's not until we give it over to the Lord that we begin to recognize the devil's tactic to trip us up, especially when he wants to tear down the marriage of someone who is trying to live for God, or those who haven't come to know who they are in Christ Jesus. Once the enemy knows you can't see the big picture, he can sneak up on you with his many lies, tricks, and schemes. I call this being spiritually blind, which gives Satan room to run rampant in our lives.

In this book, I am sharing a continuation of God's plans for my life and how He continued to walk me down the path of my purpose. It wasn't clear to me until I got backed up into a corner because I was unaware of what was happening. I got to a place where I felt like I'd hit my lowest point. I thought I was confident, but I was wavering quite a bit. I had a moment where I couldn't see what was taking place, but through fasting and prayer, I was able to find my way back to the reality of spiritual warfare. Before, things were foreign to me, but now the eyes of my spiritual understanding are open.

God gave me peace and perspective when things were chaotic because of this new understanding. "Peace I leave with you, My Peace I give unto you: not as the world giveth, give I unto you. Let not your heart be troubled, neither let it be afraid" **John 14:27, KJV**. His peace is the peace that surpasses all understanding. God could have allowed me to learn these things in and through a different situation. Instead, I had to learn what the scripture in **Isaiah 55:8-9** says, which is, "For my thoughts are not your thoughts, neither are your ways, My Ways, saith The LORD. For as the heavens are higher than the earth, so are my ways higher than your ways, and my thoughts than your thoughts."

I came to the revelation that God was preparing me for something bigger than I could have imagined. I was a bit perplexed along the way because it didn't make any sense to me at first. To be honest, it still doesn't make sense to me now. We're talking about an ordinary Sista, who is just trying to make life a little easier for herself, you know? I was going through day-to-day living life as a wife, mom, and faithful servant of God who attended church. Sure, I encouraged others, but then I went on my merry way. But hey, who am I to tell God that His Way of thinking is the wrong way? After all, He created me for ***His Purpose***, and He knows me better than I know myself, *right*?

So, my brother or sister, I'd like you to get comfortable again, but before you do, grab yourself something to snack on. Get you a soda or some punch...*(I am not even touching that one, LOL)*, or better yet, grab a pen, paper, or your journal to take notes, and then get comfortable.

Now, let's begin this phase of my life by meeting the man who would become my husband. This *will get very interesting!* If you are facing anything similar to what I have, I pray that you will receive some strategies on how to fight the enemy in the *name of Jesus!*

CHAPTER ONE

New Life Being Married

After it sunk in that I had taken an interest in this man when I came back to my church ***(My Safe Haven, I had been gone for over a year),*** I was in total shock for some reasons.

Number one, I could not understand why he was in my spirit; I did not even know his name to begin with.

Number two, I had never had this kind of experience before, where I felt that I was being hassled or harassed in my sleep over someone I didn't know. I tossed and turned for two weeks behind this man.

Number three, We attended the same church. If a relationship formed and didn't work out, it would be awkward, especially knowing his family at this point. Yet and still, I kept asking God, what was so special about this person? Why was he on my mind like this? It did not make any sense to me.

That's not all; we are talking about a guy that was way beyond my height---a human-sized teddy bear, and here I am, a bit on the petite side and didn't have a clue what to do with someone of his stature. However, my curiosity got the best of me, so I did something I had never done before in my life. I inquired about a grown man.

Yes, I was an adult, but I looked younger than I was at that time. I probably looked like a little girl standing next to him. I went to who I thought was a reliable source, and they indicated that this man was what I had observed and expected, as far as character, integrity, and mannerism was concerned. It went along with what I believed the Lord had revealed to me about this man. Although I did not know all the details, the source said that he was, in fact, an all-around good guy. I had never been this bold, but I felt like, at the very least, the mature thing to do was first to pray and go from there.

A couple of months later, we were introduced to one another. This was beyond anything I would have ever done in my entire adult life. You talk about Sista girl praying! The Lord knew that I did not know what I was doing. It would be years later before I realized that the Holy Spirit had led me to at least find out what was behind my curiosity. Remember, it took a while to understand the Holy Spirit and how He operated.

Fast forward, a couple of years later. That man I had been curious about, well, he is now my husband of thirteen years. Sorry, this testimony is not about my marriage "per se" or about a romance made in Heaven. However, the things that have occurred over the years, being married to my husband, plays a huge part in what I am about to share with you and how it looks like we are walking out God's original purpose for our lives.

So many things have occurred during the years, I'm still not sure which way to start this story. Let's just say that I was going to learn to be that wife in Proverbs 31 or 1 Corinthians 7, the way the Scripture tells us, or I was going to be that wife who is led by her own fleshly mindset. The enemy came in immediately, without me yet being aware of his tricks and tactics. Yes, I knew that the enemy could come up against your marriage, but I didn't put two and two together when he attacked us—neither did my husband. Everything happened very quickly. I didn't know that God would be using me for His Glory. In fact, I thought that was what I was doing just by being a good wife and mother—a woman who faithfully went to work and attended church. My husband, on the other hand, is considered to be a cool guy who tries to take things in strides, very cordial and reserved. He can be funny and generous when it comes to giving to others. He is a man who loves God and strives to be faithful in his walk with God. I have to say, as life moved on, some of the tests and trials we faced have altered our perspectives on our home, church, and our lives in general.

So, I am going to go back a little. A couple of months after I got married, I received a call from my mama asking me to attend a doctor's appointment on behalf of my father. The day came, and my three brothers, one from out of state, and I went to the doctor's with mama. We all had an appointment with daddy's neurologist. As the doctor began to show us the MRI results, he proceeded to explain to us that after thirty years, my daddy's tumor had come back, and this time, it was the size of a grapefruit.

If you read my first book, you will recall me sharing that my dad had surgery to remove a tumor many years ago.

Looking at the MRI scan results, you could see where the tumor was located; it was pressing towards the left side of his brain. The neurologist told us that he gave my daddy seven months to live. He wanted us to know that there was a fifty-fifty chance that he would make it given his age. If they did the surgery, they were concerned that he would not make it or be in a vegetative state for the rest of his life. The doctor asked us to make an important decision regarding the surgery. I think my mind went kind of blank. I remember us all walking out of the doctor's office, trying to be brave.

As we walked down the hallway, my daddy said the craziest thing to me. He came up behind me, being playful toward me, and said, "You are going to have a baby." I said, "No, I'm not daddy! Quit playing." He was laughing at me. I began thinking to myself, Oh, my God! What if I am pregnant? Daddy probably won't be here to see his new grandchild. I am the only girl, and I was not ready for him to go yet! I wanted him to be here to feed me like he did when I was pregnant with my oldest son. I know I kind of sound like a spoiled child right now ***(My daddy loved pregnant women; he would pamper me so well),*** but I could not handle the thought of him not being here to play with his grandkids. He was no longer going to be here to protect me. Just being in his presence had been my protection alone. So many other things came rushing to my mind. Then, all of a sudden, as we got outside preparing to get into our separate cars, I broke down and started to sob uncontrollably. I felt my heart tearing apart into little pieces.

Well, it turned out that my dad was right after all! I *was* pregnant with my second child. Months had gone by, and between one of the family members and I, we had been taking daddy to his doctor's appointments. Taking my daddy to his appointments was like going on an adventurist roller coaster ride with him. He thought it was so funny! Lol. He would give us a run for our money because he wanted to drive when he was no longer in the right state of mind. Although the tumor had caused him to lose his memory slowly, he still wanted to do things like drive on his own, but we had to kind of keep him on lockdown so that he would not do anything crazy or get lost.

I remember being about six or seven months along in my pregnancy when I took daddy to his appointment and asked him to wait outside the doctor's office building so that I could park my car. It took me some time to get from the parking structure to the building, and when I got back, my daddy was nowhere to be found. Now, I am saying to myself out loud, "Man, daddy! Don't nobody have time to be looking for you all over this building!" Knowing him, he wouldn't know where he is going. So, one of the girls that knew my daddy told me that he had gone into the right building. I waddled my big pregnant self to the elevator and guess who was riding up and down the elevator because he had forgotten where his doctor's office was located? Daddy was cracking up, but I, for one, did not find anything funny, and I was too tired to laugh!

Not long after, I went on maternity leave. My first night home, I was asleep and woke up to several missed calls. It was my mama; she called and asked if I was sitting down. I could tell that something was wrong. She told me that my daddy had disappeared. I was upset and asked questions they could not answer. Come to think of it; I should not have been surprised by what she said, as I remembered seeing a Greyhound bus ticket by accident in one of my daddy's coats jackets and had not given it any further thought at that time.

When he got to the bus station, he'd missed *that* bus; however, after my dad had been missing for about three days, he was broadcasted on a TV news station in his hometown. Thankfully, someone that had gone to high school with my dad recognized him and contacted one of my aunts to let her know that he was safe with them. I eventually found out that my little brother was home, keeping an eye on my daddy. My daddy always had something up his sleeve, and he needed to be watched. On this particular day, my daddy decided to fool my little brother into thinking that he was going to Subway, which was a couple of blocks from my parents' house, to get him a sandwich. Instead, he wrapped himself with three days' worth of clothing, hopped on a Greyhound bus, and headed to his hometown. The thing about this is my daddy was determined to get home to see his siblings and other family members. We tried to keep him from going due to his doctor's appointments. My mama decided to let him stay for a little while. We never could figure out why my daddy was so determined to go home. It wasn't very long before we found out why.

CHAPTER TWO

Losing Daddy

When it came time for me to have my baby, my dad still hadn't come home yet. After spending twenty-four hours in labor, my baby went into distress, and I had to be taken into surgery for an emergency C-section. Boy, I was so upset. But Glory be to God, I got a nine-pound, one-ounce healthy baby boy out of it!

A couple of months later, I got a call from my mama, telling me that one of my brothers was on his way to the airport to get my daddy. It was time for him to come home to receive the rest of his treatments. There was nothing else the doctors could do. He would need to be under his primary care physician. By the time my brother got to my daddy, he saw that he was not in the best condition. When my brother and daddy arrived home, my husband took our two children and me over to see him. When we got to my parent's house, I saw my dad in a way I had never seen him. He was looking very fragile and thin. I tried to be strong, but it took everything in me not to fall out in front of him.

At that moment, it all made sense to me why my daddy had wanted to go back to his hometown. He knew that he did not have much time left here. My husband handed our baby to my dad to take a family photo. This was the first time that he got to see his new grandbaby; remember, this is the one that he knew was coming, but I did not know that this would be the last time my daddy would see him.

About an hour later, my mama and I decided to get my dad to the Emergency room. Since I worked in the Emergency room at a local hospital, I was able to call and explain the situation to one of my ER doctors. She requested for us to bring him in immediately. When we got to the hospital, they had a bed already waiting for him. The doctor I worked with did an amazing job caring for my dad, and the neurologist was already there to examine my daddy, which was really quick considering any other day. It looked like my dad was having a series of mini strokes. They admitted him immediately. My daddy spent two weeks in the hospital, and I went there almost every day to see him before he was sent to a hospice facility.

My middle brother from out of state had flown in by the following week. He made it down, but he could not muster up the courage to see our dad when he arrived. I went to speak with him, but he was in such a bad state of mind that he just could not deal with all that was happening with our daddy. It would be at the very last minute that he finally went to see him. On the other hand, my oldest brother did his best to be strong. It was a blur for everybody. Family from all over the place had come to see my dad. My aunts and uncles had flown in as well, along with others that we knew, who were like family, church family, my dad's Pastor, and his wife came to see him as well.

At that time, my younger brother had gotten into a situation that prevented him from seeing my dad. He could only express his love and say his goodbyes via phone. The hospice nurse came in to explain what to expect from someone who was *transitioning.* While we all gathered around my dad, I expressed to her my dad's role in our lives. He was a strong, caring, loving husband, father, grandfather, brother, uncle, son, friend, and cook.

I went home to get some rest. Later in the middle of the night, while I was asleep, my cousin Ella called me; when I answered, she asked to speak with my husband. When I gave him the phone, I just knew that whatever it was that my cousin did not dare to tell me herself. My daddy had gone on to be with the Lord. At that moment, I don't recall shedding tears. I just remember getting myself together to go to the convalescent home to see my daddy, one last time. When I got there, I saw my mama and other family members gathered around my daddy. We all hugged one another. My mama and I held on to each other, and we let daddy know that we would see him later.

It came time for my daddy's funeral service, which was held at my home church. I remember breastfeeding my baby, but no milk would come out. My milk supply had dried up. I also remember attempting to do something with my hair and soon realized that I was bald on both sides of my head. I had internalized my emotions, but it was the only way to cope without falling apart. I was so stressed that my body had taken a hit without realizing it but thank God a Sista girl knew how to do her hair because there was no time to go to the beauty salon! It was already late at night, and my dad's homegoing service was in the morning. I managed to hide the bald spots without anyone knowing. I didn't want to tell my mama for fear of her worrying too much. At this point, my goal was to try and remain as calm as possible. Furthermore, one of my daddy's wishes was to be buried in his hometown next to his brother, so we had to hold a second homegoing service there as well.

My family and I booked a flight out to my daddy's hometown that following weekend. My husband was gracious enough to stay back home with our children. This second homegoing service hit me harder than the first one. When it came time to view my dad's body, to give my final farewell, what I had been trying to avoid, happened anyway. I went into a severe state of anxiety. Honestly, one of the things I hate doing the most is showing my vulnerability, especially in front of a crowd. But I could only be strong for so long. However, this time, I was no longer going to see him alive. It was time to lay my daddy's body to rest. Yes, I know! I know that my father went home to be with the Lord, but he's been my daddy my whole life. I believe he felt that he was leaving me in good hands since I was married. Still, I had to find a way to deal with not being able to see him for however long the Lord leaves me here on this earth.

My most memorable moment of my daddy was his last doctor's appointment that I had taken him to. We pulled up in his driveway, and he gave me a happy belated birthday card with a twenty-dollar bill in it. It read, "I love you." I cried, and he laughed and kissed me. I told him that I loved him too. I am so glad that God gave us that moment. Still, till this day, I find myself alone, crying from time to time, because although he is here in my heart, it is during my most difficult seasons since he has been gone that I longingly wished I could go to him, and cry on his shoulders, so that he can tell me, "Aww girl! What are you crying for? *(He would laugh at this point),* and say, everything is going to be alright!" After my father's passing, the Lord blessed my husband and I, and we were able to move into our new home.

My husband had it in his heart to adopt my oldest son so that he, too, could have our last name and not feel left out. We would be a whole family with the same last name. Years before my husband and I married, one of the things that I had requested from the Lord was that if He allowed me a second chance to be married, that this person would be a good father figure to my son, that he would be loved as if he was their own. I didn't know that adoption would be a part of the equation, so you can imagine my gratitude towards my Heavenly Father. It was an answer to my prayer that was now manifested, and God was being glorified!! We went through the adoption process, and our families on both sides were there to witness a beautiful occasion. I believe it was one of the happiest moments of my son's life.

CHAPTER THREE

Losing My Little Brother

It would be about two years later that another devastation would hit our family. It was a weekend that I had to work. My husband, our boys and I had been in church all day that Sunday. We had 11 a.m. and 3:30 p.m. services; after that, I rushed home, hoping to get a quick nap before I went into work for my graveyard shift. About an hour in a half later, I got a call from my mama, telling me that my brother had passed out and might need to go to the hospital. They already had the paramedics there to observe him and felt he didn't need to be taken to the hospital via ambulance. But my mama asked me if I could call and make my charge nurse aware that they would be bringing him in for observation? After making the call, I tried to go back to sleep. I was extremely exhausted due to working the night before but I tossed and turned the entire time. I remained restless until I had to get up and get ready for work.

Before I could sit down at my workstation, one of the doctors that had been evaluating my brother came up to me with a look of concern on her face. She asked, "Is that your brother that you called in for?" I answered, "Yes, that's my brother!" She said she had just gotten his test results back and that his body was shutting down at that very moment. She told me if his body did not respond to the medication, she would have to intubate him.

This is a process in which they insert a tube through the person's mouth and then into their airway. This would allow my brother to be placed on a ventilator to assist him in breathing. I felt this feeling of anxiousness come over me. I looked over at my coworkers; there were two of them. One was just finishing her shift and was going to give us a report; instead, she said she would stay for a while until things were more stable with my brother, but things went from *calm* to being overwhelming.

I went over to my mama to give her some comfort, but the look on her face told me that we were about to have a long night. I told her what the doctor had told me. I could hear the fear in her voice, and I thought, she's trying to stay as calm as possible. We both went over to my brother while they were inserting the IVs and administering his medication. He was still having a hard time breathing. I stepped away for a second to let my coworkers know that I would be at the bedside. At this time, my mama said she could hear him reciting the 23rd Psalm.

My mama told him that she was going to call our aunts, uncle, and grandmother. He said, "Mama! Don't leave me by myself!" Mama told him, "I'll be right back son, I'm just going to smoke a cigarette and call your auntie and grandmother to let them know your status. Your sister will be with you, and I will be right back." I stepped back to my brother's bedside, and I noticed that he still had difficulty breathing independently. He looked at me and laid his head on my arm. He said, "Hey Nik," between breaths. I said, "Hey yourself, little brother." I tried to reassure him. I said, "Try and remain calm; God's got you." By that time, the doctor came into the room (my little brother and I were the only ones in the room, my mama hadn't made it back yet) and said, "The fluid in his lungs is what's prohibiting him from breathing. We're going to have to intubate him immediately."

A couple of nurses, a respiratory therapist, and some techs all came to prepare my brother for intubation. Just as they were doing this, mama walked in, and reality sunk in. Little by little, you could see and feel panic beginning to rise. At this point, I had no time to fall out; there was no time to cry or to freak out—my only concern was my mama, so I had to be strong. The doctor asked us to step out of the room. At that moment, I knew I was going to need some help with mama, so I ran quickly to a nearby phone to call my oldest brother. I told him that the doctors were getting ready to intubate our brother and asked if he could make it down to the hospital. Unfortunately, his wife was out of town, and he was alone with his brand-new baby. I said, "Okay, I would call him back." I called my grandmother, and she said they were on their way. I asked her to please hurry so they could help me with mama, and she said, "Okay, we are coming." I called my husband to tell him what was happening, and I asked him to please pray.

I walked my mama into the hallway, put her up against the wall, and wrapped my arms around her tightly. At that moment, two of my coworkers came over to us and wrapped their arms around us both. All four of us were up against the wall. We were all trying to comfort my mama and give her the strength she needed, but the anxiety was getting worse and worse. You could feel her weight getting heavier, the longer it took them to finish doing what they needed to do. The doctor finally came to see us and the look on her face told us all that it was not going to end the way we wanted it to. She said that we should prepare ourselves to see my little brother. We all went to my little brother's bedside; he had tubes all over his body. It looked as if every ER doctor on duty, every tech, nurse, therapist, and about fifteen others were trying to save my little brother's life. All you could hear was my mama, asking me over and over again,

"Why?" She said, "God, you took my husband, and now, you are taking my son, God! Why?" Then, she would turn to me and repeat the same question. All I could say was, "I don't know." I didn't have an answer at that very moment. All I felt was pain and sorrow. There was not a dry eye in the room when I looked up. Just then, my aunt, uncle, and grandmother arrived, but it was too late... ***my little brother was gone.***

I had to make that dreadful call to both my brothers. I felt so heavy and burdened down. I called my oldest brother first. I told him that our little brother didn't make it. I imagined what he looked like on the other side of the phone. He asked a couple of questions and said, "Okay, thank you for letting me know." I told him that I would call our other brother. I made the call to our other brother, and when I told him, I didn't hear a peep at the other end of the phone. I think my sister-in-law had to take the phone from him to get the details, but there was nothing else to say. I called my husband to inform him of my brother's passing. You could hear the solemn tone in his voice. He said that he would be praying for us.

Mama and I had to go through the necessary process of filling out paperwork to allow some privacy for our family to come in and say their farewells and then send the body to the morgue. It felt like we were there all night, but everything happened within a two to three-hour time span. It just seemed like my little brother, and I didn't have enough time. If someone were to ask *for what?* I'm not sure, maybe hanging out as we used to, laughing about stuff our daddy used to do, talking about how much we loved Jesus and how good the Lord was to us! There was no more time; he was so young, only 29 years old. He was taken away from us so soon. First, it was my daddy, then my little brother; both were gone within two years apart. My brother was my kids' uncle who loved all of his nieces and nephews, that was for sure. Eventually, we all went home. By this time, I was completely drained and worn out. My husband was up waiting for me. It was then that I was able to let out some of my grief. The whole thing was just so surreal to me.

I hadn't slept all morning. My husband had to go to work, so my best friend made her way down to support me. There was so much support from all over. My brother was loved and liked by so many people. The doctors and my friends from work were also incredibly supportive. Many who attended to my brother at the hospital that night were affected by it. I took some time off to recuperate and even went to counseling with my mama before returning to work.

CHAPTER FOUR

God, Where Are You?

Life as we knew it had to go on. I found myself trying to juggle being a wife, a mother to two boys, and working the night shift. We would go about our normal lives, going to church as usual. But then, one Sunday, during service, I was sitting in the audience listening to the Pastor preaching when I happened to look over where my husband was sitting. I saw that something was happening with him; it was as if he was puzzled and trying to figure something out. *Suddenly*, a look of submission came over him.

After service was over, he told me that he needed to talk. When the church was cleared out, he sat down next to me and shared the revelation he had gotten from the Lord. After he told me what happened, he said something like, "I have accepted my call to preach" *(I'm paraphrasing)*. He asked, "Do you have any objection to this?" I am looking at him and thinking, what am I supposed to do with that?! Tell God, No?" I don't want God to strike *ME* down if I say no! Lol I said, "Well, if that's what you feel God is calling you to do, then I stand by your decision." I encouraged him and told him that I believed he could do it.

This reminded me of what I thought before we got married.

Remember, I told you I thought he would be someone important? I knew he loved God; I just didn't know that he would become a minister. Little did we know the minute my husband said, ***"Yes Lord, send me I'll go"*** we were going in for more than what we bargained for! We didn't know that we were about to go on a long, ***hard*** ride. This road was so far ahead of us; we could not have seen it or have known what was coming!

My brother or sister here is a transparent moment. When I think about it, I'd only been married for three years, and quite of few things had already taken place. My daddy and little brother passed away and I was already feeling kind of drained.

Things were slowly unraveling in my household right before my eyes. I felt as if I was getting hit left and right, and one day; I just had to stop and ask myself, what was going on in the world? Nothing was making sense to me. We were already having issues with my oldest son, whom God had given the gift of singing. On top of all of this, my husband and I had become unusually strained and was having communication issues. With all the things that had taken place over the last three or four years, I had to admit that my communication with God seemed to be at a dry place as well. Yes, I was going to church, Bible study, doing the usual stuff, and I think I talked to God a lot. The real question is, was it enough for God? It certainly did not feel like it was.

You see, when you have two people who love God come together as a family, know that the enemy will do whatever it takes to separate them. I was unaware that the enemy was watching us from a mile away. Yes, we may know some of the adversary's tricks and what he is capable of doing, but when you are not careful, you can find yourself leaving doors open that you did not intend to leave open. I thought that as a wife, I could handle trying to resolve issues and conflicts with my husband by sitting down and discussing our situations as mature men and women do. Well, that didn't work. You see, when one spouse believes in something so strongly, you cannot get them to see the whole picture.

Something went wrong somewhere along the way, and now there was an increase of communication breakdowns. There was a lot of confusion and misunderstandings, simply put, chaos was running rampant throughout the household!

At one point I thought I would have a nervous breakdown, and the fact that I worked graveyard shift didn't make it any better. I was getting calls from my oldest child's school almost every day about him fidgeting in his chair and not sitting still or getting up to sharpen his pencil too many times. It was mind-boggling that the teachers couldn't handle a few of these things, but we are in a different time than when I was coming up, so I had to keep rolling with everything coming my way. This prevented me from getting proper sleep. My sleep patterns were not consistent, so I used every chance I could to get some sleep.

One night, something so unexpected happened in our home. I was at work when I got a call from my husband to tell me that the police were there, with someone from the D.C.F.S (Department of Child and Family Services). They wanted to speak with me, and they were prepared to take our children out of the home if necessary. This was the worst thing anyone, especially I, could hear as a mother! You know, in the past, I'd had many instances that happened to me that would make you go crazy if it were your child.

There were many times I felt like my heart was going to pop out of my chest; this ***was one of them!!!***

I happen to be the only person working the desk this specific night. It should have been two of us, but things were changing at our job, so I was left to work alone. My charge nurse was speaking with one of our doctors. I tried to respect their time and position, but time was of the essence for me. I urgently and politely grabbed my charge nurse by the arm and told her that there was an emergency at home, that I had to leave. I did not wait for her response, and I had no time for any questions. I gave her a report of what needed to be done to carry on with the work. I left her standing right there, not caring who would take over the desk. At that time, I did not care! I ran out of the door, with my heart beating super hard. During the drive home, I kept saying, "Jesus! ***The Blood of Jesus!"*** repeatedly.

What usually took me about ten minutes on the freeway to get home took me about half that time to arrive. ***(Thank God, I didn't get stopped by the police).*** I walked into my house with the caseworker waiting for me. We sat down, and he explained that an anonymous call had been made about a suspicious story my son had told to another child that another student overheard and relayed to an adult teacher. The whole thing was so far-fetched and crazy; I felt this could have been cleared up in another way. I believe this was part of the enemy's plan to create havoc in our family.

We did not come together in prayer as a family should. Therefore, I feel that it caused some resentment and bitterness. We may have prayed individually, but need I remind you that there is power when we come together as a family. The problem was that the communication between my husband and I was going downhill. Yup, the enemy had gained a big foothold in our home!

So, we had a child doing all kinds of crazy stuff at school who was not doing the same things at home but was doing stuff that did not make any sense to me. He is an intelligent kid; something just wasn't right! Here I was, trying to juggle this thing called life all at the same time, but I was getting nowhere near a resolution. I would ask God the same question over again, "God, what is going on? Why are things so crazy? Nothing is making any sense! Lord, what is going on?"

We spent the next couple of years going through so many ups and downs. It seemed to be more downs than ups! I was in a place of confusion. I remember sitting in the back room of my house for days, thinking about my family and how we were falling apart, but I could not understand how, why, or what was happening to us. We were still in the beginning stage of being a whole family; what was causing these problems? I replayed things over in my mind and still could not figure out what had triggered this ongoing cycle. Everything around me was beginning to be too much. But still, I had to keep it moving as much as I could. I was asking God to sustain my family. I was beginning to feel that there was something more that I needed to do, *but what?* I had no clue what to ask or even say to God at this point. I kept feeling like something was missing, something was off, something was not quite right. And because I serve a big God, I knew there was a solution somewhere. But what was I to do in the meantime?

One Sunday, we had a program at church, and unexpectedly, my son had to sing that day. Usually, he would have the choir to back him, but this time, he sang his first solo, **"His Eye Is on The Sparrow."** This version was sung by the Mississippi Children's

Choir featuring Bryan Wilson. It was the first time we had heard him sing this song. He and I had listened to this song many times in the car, but I didn't know that he could listen to a song and know how to sing it. He was asked to sing this song that he had not rehearsed. I asked him if he knew the song. He said, "Yes, mom! I know the song." I told him, "You know, you can always sing a song that you know." He convinced me that he knew the song. "I said okay, go ahead."

My brother or sister, this was the first time the Lord revealed why I was having such a hard time with this child since all the chaos broke out. As he was singing, you could see almost everyone standing up on their feet, cheering him on. I had to stand still because I was recording him. Right in the middle of him singing, I felt I heard the Holy Spirit say to me, "The reason you are having a hard time with him is because he is anointed." My son was about ten years old; I knew that the enemy was after him right then. He didn't know who he was yet or how to fight against the enemy. He didn't even know how to pray for himself. I heard the Spirit of God say, "You will have to fight for him. You will have to stand in the gap on his behalf."

Once I heard the Lord speak to me concerning my child, it was as if a light bulb had switched on. I knew then that something in me was happening. Even though I was still annoyed with our circumstances, I began to see my son a little bit differently. With this new revelation, I figured that I would be able to share this piece of information with my husband, except that we were not on the same page. I could not understand why. Surely, husbands and wives have their ups and downs and work out their differences. So, why couldn't we do that? We were at a standstill. I just didn't understand and kept asking, "God, why? What am I doing wrong?"

During the next season, we encountered more chaos. My husband and I decided for my side of the family to help with our situation concerning our son. As the saying goes, it takes a village to raise a child. At least, that was part of our thought process. But for me, considering what I had already gone through with my family in earlier years regarding how protective they can be towards my son, I was not in favor of involving them with our problems. Still, at the same time, I also knew that they loved this child too. We had a family meeting, although I really wasn't feeling this idea, we decided to allow my oldest son to live with my mama. Well, let me tell you, it was one of the worst decisions ever made and also one of the most humbling experiences I've ever had.

The few weeks we all spent going back and forth, trying to help my son realize and appreciate that he had a mother, father, a good home, and family that cared about him, actually turned out to be one of the biggest family fights I've ever encountered. My motherhood was questioned, and things were said that hurt me to the core. I felt that some of my family had turned their backs on me. I wasn't given a chance to explain my position. In all honesty, I didn't feel I knew what my position was anymore. I remember explaining what was said to my husband regarding my motherhood, but there was a look on his face that told me that he wasn’t on my side either. I stopped in my tracks; I said to myself, "Oh my God! I’m in this thing all by myself." You mean to tell me that I don't know my position as a wife either!

I was tired of feeling burdened down all of the time. I am usually a strong, positive, and resilient person. I don't let everything get to me that easily. In this case, everything that could come against me came simultaneously. I actually felt like giving up. I wanted to just walk away from it all! I wanted to walk away from being a wife and even a mother because the enemy had me feeling as if I couldn't do anything right. It seemed as if there was no solution in sight! I felt like the walls were closing in on me! On one side of the wall, my family was coming against me; on the other side, my husband and I were struggling to get on one accord, and on top of that, I was trying to figure out what was happening with my son. I felt like I wasn't getting the help I needed from anyone, so the arrangement we had was unnecessary. I packed my son's thing's from my mama's house; and from there, I shut down and distanced myself from my family. By this time, they were driving me to drink! I was ready to drink a whole bottle of Hennessy, ***literally***!

If all of that wasn't enough, a couple of weeks later my husband and I were called into a meeting with our son's school principal. We were told that someone found a letter written by my son that they felt would threaten the school. Considering the nature of the situation, the school felt compelled to investigate further. They suggested that our son be admitted into a facility and put on a 72-hour hold. During that time his mental state and behavior would be evaluated but that quickly changed. They went on to extend the time to 14 more days because he yelled out to another patient to stop making fun of him. Now, how much worse could it get from here? I am now asking, ***"GOD, WHERE ARE YOU???!!!"*** I cried almost every day having to go to see him in that place. I had no idea why I felt like I was fighting so hard and at the same time, it was if I was fighting thin air! I was just swinging in the air and not hitting anything! I made a decision to take a couple of weeks off from work until I could get this situation under control.

The first day my husband and I visited him, my husband cried; he could not handle seeing him there. My husband felt that seeing my son there was like seeing him in a hospital bed, but I was ready to roll up my sleeves! It was time to fight the enemy back, and I began to fast and pray on behalf of my son! Within those fourteen days, my son was able to have visitations and phone call privileges, and one of those calls was from all the choir members from the church. There was so much support from them. They missed him and wanted to encourage him. They asked him to sing something for them while he was on the speaker where everyone could hear him. He broke out with a couple of verses of **"Never would have made it**," by Marvin Sapp, then he paused for a second and picked up on, **"I would have lost it all, but now I see how you were there for me."** By the time he finished singing, everyone was in tears. It seemed that everyone was encouraged by him although he was in the situation himself!

Let me pause here; I remember back when I was pregnant with him, I used to put headphones on my belly and play gospel music pretty much every day, sometimes, for hours and hours. He would wake up for his feeding around midnight when he was about one or two months old. Remember those old-school VHS cassette tapes we had back in the early 2000s? Well, I had one with Donnie McClurkin Live in London and one with Fred Hammond's Radical for Christ Purpose by Design. I think each of them was an hour-long concert, and my son would stay up and listen to both of them for two hours, then he would fall asleep on the very last song. I don't recall how long I played those tapes. Those became some very calm and peaceful night feedings. He made it so easy for me during those nights. Then, I began to wonder more about why I was being reminded of this? It just seemed so crazy what was happening, and the timing of all of this seemed so important. The Lord reminded me that

He had a special anointing on my son's life. However, he would have to make that choice for himself to follow Christ fully.

During the time he was admitted, I started doing some research. I had seen this too many times before working in a hospital, I knew that medication would probably be considered but, I didn't want the doctors to prescribe him any medication. We had a meeting with the physician who was seeing him, and I was prepared for him to tell me that my son should be put on medication. I did not care if he was a doctor. I knew what the Lord had already told me concerning my son. It wasn't going to be, "If push came to shove, then we would give him the medications," or "Let's just try giving him the medication for a couple of weeks"; I was not having it! Well, just as I expected, the doctor suggested that my son be put on medication. I was so upset because for one, the doctor was very impersonal and he didn't give him a thorough examination. It felt like he was just going through a routine and made a decision. On top of that, he couldn't even give an explanation as to why he made the suggestion to medicate him. So, I had some things I needed to get off of my chest. I expressed them with him until my husband cut in to try and simmer things down.

That same day my husband and I returned from visiting our son at the facility, I was approached by someone who then inquired about the idea of medicating him. I was taken back because I didn't ever recall having this conversation with them as it was a private matter. I say this because you don't know if people genuinely care about you or your children, or if they are pretending to be concerned for you, so that they can go back and gossip or spread lies. I told this person that there was nothing wrong with him; he didn't need to take medication. I had a responsibility to care for this child. I told this person, if I were to let them prescribe him medicine and later find out he didn't need the drugs, I would be mad at myself and everyone else involved with that decision; therefore, I would not be letting him take drugs that could potentially ruin his young mind.

Not long after my son was released, he woke up one morning with a dream and wanted to tell his father and I. He said he was on a boat in a Safari River near a waterfall. He said it was four people, one he recognized as his friend, but the other two were faceless. He told us that Jesus spoke to him, he could hear Him, but he could not see His face. He said Jesus said to him, "You can die now and go to Heaven, or you can stay here and go to hell?" He said, "I want to die now and go to Heaven." He said that just then, he was lifted up by the Holy Spirit above the boat into the air, and he saw the boat go down the waterfall. He was about twelve years old. When he told us about this dream, we both knew that he was speaking the truth. Even today, I believe that my son will one day understand what this dream means and that it will come into manifestation soon; I believe that he will get the full significance of what that dream truly means for him.

By this time, I could sense in the spirit that I was being viewed as crazy simply because I shared with some close to me what the Lord said concerning my son. He told me there was nothing wrong with him. To others it seemed as if I was only trying to protect my sons image, but this was the time the Lord was revealing himself to me in ways I had never experienced before. I was hearing His voice very clearly and it didn't make sense to anyone around me during that time. Quite frankly, I didn't have time to focus on that because my husband and I were still at odds with one another and our son was still going through all these issues. I was going back and forth to counseling for my oldest son, and I still had to work and go to church as if everything was all right. It was an ongoing cycle with no end in sight but my eyes were opening up to the fact that there was more to these situations we were facing then we could see. This was a spiritual battle and it was going to take the army of the Lord to help get these things corrected. "For we wrestle not against flesh and blood, but against principalities, against powers, against rulers of the darkness of this world, against spiritual wickedness in high places…" **Ephesians 6:12, KJV**

CHAPTER FIVE

In The Boxing Ring

The enemy had me in a place where I was trying to figure out the point of my existence but in reality, there was something on the inside of me that I had not known existed quite yet. I felt so down on myself that I almost forgot the person I was. When you get to a place that others close to you feel a certain way about you, and it's not positive in their eyes, you ***almost*** start to believe it.

For instance, you question what you recall when you're called a liar, but you also know you've told the truth to the best of your knowledge. You start to think you're the problem when you're told you're the problem, although you don't fully understand what the problem is. You may question yourself if you're told *you're fake*, but then you snap out of those lies because the truth is, all you know how to be is your true self. You may question your walk with God when statements are made such as, "You ***think*** *you* are "Holy," but you must remember where He brought you from and that your **desire** is to live for Him.

When you finally get to a place where you genuinely want to serve God whole heartily, but others are looking at you like ***yeahhhhh rightttt*** while saying, "You know you are doing too much?" You have to reject the lies of the enemy.

Listen, my brother or sister; Satan will have you in a battle for *your* mind. I finally discovered that I was in a boxing ring with the enemy fighting on behalf of my spouse, children, myself, and my church. But I also found myself fighting with them instead of *for* them. In some cases, I was oblivious to the fact that other outsiders were more aware of my situation than I was. What's so funny about all of this is that everyone who was aware was trying their hardest to pretend like they didn't know what I was going through. I was in a battle!

At some point, I started to wonder why I was feeling so mentally and sometimes emotionally tired all of the time. It's because the battle that I have been fighting all this time was not my battle to fight alone. That is how the distractions, confusion, feelings of hurt, and misunderstandings came in. There was a whole lot of conversations taking place that I was not aware of, and yet, I was in the boxing ring, fighting a fight that I did not know I was fighting, until I got in that place of asking questions like, "Lord, what is happening? Why is all of this happening? What did I do to deserve this? I understand that I may have gotten upset and fallen short when I should have handled certain situations better. I understand that we should have prayed about the situation together, but nobody wants to pray together anymore, so I am left to deal with this the best way I know how, *alone*, behind closed doors. Lord, Help!"

I understand that husbands and wives should talk things out to better understand each other; unfortunately, when you've come into a marriage with a broken, wounded, and rejected spirit, you find yourself operating under these different spirits. When you don't deal with the past, you claim the baggage, and it will manifest in your relationships.

Baggage of hurt, so you shut down.

Baggage of all types of rejection, so you shut down,

Baggage of a result of being set in your ways, you take on a this is how it's going to be attitude, so you shut down.

Baggage of insecurities, so you shut down.

Baggage of being molested, so you shut down.

Baggage of not being valued, so you shut down because it's the only way you know how to filter through all negative energy.

I found myself so burdened down, and I realized that the pre-marital counseling we had should have been more extensive in preparing us for a lifelong marriage after we said I do. Mind you, my brother or sister, some of us still don't know what's inside of us yet, and for others, you thought you knew, but it is not until you have been faced with many challenges that you come to find out what ***it*** is. I found myself so busy fighting in the ring with the enemy that I forgot who I was before I got married. All because I had not gotten the full revelation of who I was in Christ Jesus. Yet, I was still in the boxing ring, trying to fight this fight that wasn't mine to fight alone.

Here is the crazy thing, these battles were at different stages of my journey. I would get strengthened and then I would be confused all over again. Yes, I knew it was the enemy; I just didn't know the direction the attack was coming from, but the Lord was helping me get back to a place of clarity, and the fog was beginning to clear. I started to see the direction I was going; it was Jesus who was and still is interceding for me while seated at the Father's right hand **(Roman 8:34, KJV)**. Glory be to God!

I had to put on my armor and speak to God! I had my weapon of prayer, which started with "Lord, what is going on? Then He would give me an answer in His word that says, "The Lord is my light and my salvation, whom shall I fear, the Lord is the strength of my life; of whom shall I be afraid? When the wicked, even mine enemies and my foes, came upon me to eat up my flesh, they stumbled and fell," **Psalms 21:1-2, KJV.** It was scriptures like this that gave me hope.

Then, I started to sort things out in my mind, asking myself, okay, who is my enemy? What is the enemy after? Why is the enemy after what he is after? Something clicked inside of me, this thing was not happening just to be happening; there was a reason. So, I asked the Lord, what is the reason? Give me something to work with? The Lord gave me another answer. He said, "There is a gift that I have put inside of you; go find it and when you find it, open it."

Now, I am back in the boxing ring, regaining my strength back because now, I am beginning to understand that there is something for me to fight for (my purpose), and something to fight with (a different, deeper, and strategic prayer life) this time. I now know that the Spirit of the Lord is working with me. I know that He's fighting for me against the adversary, the one that did not want me to know that I have something worth fighting for. **Hallelujah**!

I found out there was a gift inside me that I needed to unlock, but Satan does not want me to open it because he knows that he will lose the battle once it is open. Now that I had a little more strength, I could clothe myself in my weapons of warfare; I put on prayer and fasting. It cost me hunger, but I was gaining more knowledge and understanding of what was going on in my surroundings. The enemy threw so many fiery darts at me; I was only able to duck and dodge him for so long. This happened during the times I was looking in the wrong direction. Sometimes, the enemy could be right in your face, and you won't know it if you aren't careful, or prayerful.

CHAPTER SIX

The Fire Inside Of Me

I'm now seeing that this was a huge spiritual battle, and here I was, trying to fight this thing in the natural. I could now see that the enemy had gotten his creepy, nasty hands on my family. With my husband being a minister and all, you'd think that he would have recognized this as well. But he didn't see it, or better yet, it seemed like I was the enemy. He was going through his spiritual battlc, asidc from us. I startcd reading and studying the Word of God more. I started having this urge to pray more often than I used to. So much so that God would not leave me alone about it. By the grace of God, I believe that I was being birthed as an intercessor.

Now, this is where things get a little more interesting. One day, I had asked my husband if we could pray together. It was a bold move on my part. Here's the thing my brother or sister, I always prayed to God alone because I had never really developed the practice of praying aloud in public. Somehow, I had acquired this fear of praying in front of people. It wasn't something I was comfortable with doing. So, when I asked my husband if we could come together and pray, he said, you go ahead and lead the prayer. Now, I'm thinking to myself, I really wanted you to pray for us. Instead, he made me pray out loud. The Lord knows I was so nervous. I was one of those girls that would break out into a cold sweat; I'm talking about, from my forehead and under my armpits. Normally, anybody that would ask me to pray would barely get a word out of me. My mouth would stay shut, and my mind would go blank. It was just one of those experiences I had a hard time with. I didn't care to pray out loud in front of many people—this went on for thirty-seven years.

But something changed. After I prayed, I got a response from my husband that I was not expecting; he said, "You can't manipulate God with your prayers." Again, I was in such a state of confusion. What did he mean by "Manipulate God?" Well, I went straight into my room, got down on my knees, and asked God, "What did my husband mean? I can't manipulate you! You are God; you do whatever You want to do. Why did he say that? I have come to you my whole life; you have answered many of my prayers. I don't understand why my husband said what he said, it doesn't make any sense."

It would be years later before I would pray in front of him again. I began to seek God; I mean this whole thing was so draining for me, I couldn't get a handle on anything. I was looking for answers; I was beginning to feel like I was in a *twilight zone.* I don't really care for that show, but this was exactly what my life was starting to feel like.

My husband was being ordained as a minister, which caused quite a stir. At that time, our church was looking for someone to fill the role of Senior Pastor. Some were not happy that my husband was being considered. We were ***already*** in a crazy whirlwind! The tension between us was at an all-time high. Because he loves God, I thought he would take what we were about to commit to seriously and have a change of heart about how we were both acting at home. It was important that we at least try to fix things between us as we stood before God and the church. I tell you; we had no idea the enemy was so upset about what was going to take place, and as a result, he was trying to wreak more havoc on our family! What was strange is, the more distant we became as husband and wife, the closer I was drawing nearer to God.

"And we know that all things work together for good to them that love God, to them who are the called according to His purpose." **Romans 8:28, KJV**

I decided to reach out to a ninety-year-old mother from another church for prayer. She had such a sweet spirit. A friend of mine told me about her. I told her what I was going through, and she set a time to pray and minister to me throughout the week. She was like my mentor. One evening, she surprised me and told me to pray. I looked at the phone like, you want me to pray. Out loud? I'm saying things to myself like, I do not pray aloud like that. But like an obedient child, I did what she asked me to do. This ninety-year-old mother of the church started me into **"the praying out loud business"** after losing my confidence. That was all I needed to light the fire that was already on the inside of me! This went on for several months before other changes had taken place. She went home to be with the Lord a few years later; may she rest in peace. Amen.

Now, my husband is the one who initially had me praying out loud, but I thank God that He used her to ignite that fire in me, so now I can pray in front of anyone in general.

1 Corinthians 3:6 ---"I Paul have planteth, Apollos watered; but God gave the increase." **Side Note**: Paul means little or little flock --my husband planteth, - 'eth' on the end of a word means when it was first given until now-- Apollos means learned---the mother watered---then God gave the increase and lit the fire in me to pray out loud!

In the weeks following those daily phone calls, I realized that a shift had taken place. I had a friend whom I had worked with for many years. She was one of the nurses who had tried to help save my little brother's life, she too, had been affected by his death. As she developed her relationship with the Lord, she would be courageous enough to pick up the phone and give me a call to ask for prayer. The Lord would not let me off of the phone until I did as she had requested; He would put it in my heart to minister and pray for her right on the spot, whether we were in person or if we were having a conversation over the phone. After talking and ministering with her for a few weeks, she began searching for a church home; she asked if I knew of a church, she could go to? Now, to be honest, I was very reluctant to invite her to church because we were in between Pastors, and we did not have an ordained Pastor yet; we were still looking for one at that time. I told her the truth about the status of our church and that she was more than welcome to visit. She came to church that following Sunday, and since then, what I have witnessed, I am now seeing an amazing woman who is on fire and absolutely loves God!

My birthday had come and gone when my mother *(biological)* had called me to wish me a happy birthday. We talked for a little while, and I could tell that something was bothering her. So, I asked if I could pray for her? She said, "Sure." This was the first time that I prayed with my mother in her presence. I remember telling her that I didn't know any extravagant words, but I would go ahead and pray. I prayed with her; we said, "I love you" to one another, and then hung up. I believe it was about a day later when she called me, and the first thing she said to me was, "I think you are a prayer warrior." I'm looking at the phone like, *WHAT*? In my mind, I'm like, what is a prayer warrior? Lol. Yes, my brother or sister, I have heard of a prayer warrior, but really, I was trying to figure out how something like that even related to me?! Look, remember I told you all that I had not prayed out loud for thirty-seven years. I was so used to praying to myself, under my breath, quietly, with just me and God "alone." Why would God put something like that on me now? Why didn't He have me doing something like that at an earlier age? Well, thinking back on hindsight, the Lord had always been preparing me. It was His timing for me in learning to become bolder for Him.

My life was now changing swiftly. One of my spiritual mothers asked me what gift the Lord planned to use for His Glory? I was looking at her like; I don't know. I said to her, "Well, I know how to do hair!" We both started cracking up laughing because, to be honest, I didn't even think I had a spiritual gift from God for me to use. Then, it dawned on me that maybe that was why I kept feeling out of place! It just never occurred to me that there was a connection with all the things that were happening to me and my family, that He actually had a gift for me. I never inquired until one morning; I was so tired and fed up with what was happening in my household that I got down on my knees right on the living room floor in front of my sofa and began to cry out to the Lord! I said, "Lord, whatever you want me to do, I will do it. Lord, God, what is Your plan for my life? What *gift* do you have for me? I surrender my will to Your Will." I believe the Lord was causing me to take my focus off of my husband and child to focus more on Him because not doing so only made matters worse. So, my focus shifted, and I had to step my prayer time up a notch. When I finished praying, I had a snotty nose and swollen eyes.

CHAPTER SEVEN

The Vow

There was a revival taking place at my co-worker and friends' church. All my friends knew one another, so we gathered ourselves together to have a blessed time in the house of the Lord. The Evangelist that was there came from out of state. God used her in such a powerful way! The Holy Spirit spoke through her to me, and she said, "You have been wanting to give up, but you are too strong to give up." She said, "Whatever you are doing with your son, keep doing it with him; the Lord is going to give you a Spirit of prayer," she tapped one hand and said, "He will teach you and show you how." On the other hand, she tapped as well. At that time, I was having a little Bible study with my oldest son at home because I felt in my spirit that God wanted him to understand who God really is. After all, I am no teacher, nor was I a Bible scholar. I wasn't sure if I was on the right path with what I was trying to convey to him in breaking down the scriptures for him to relate to them. You see, my brother or sister, I had been seeking God's face through fasting and praying, and God gave me a word that was undeniably true. This was the first time I had seen this Evangelist, so in my mind, I'm screaming, God, you heard me! You heard me!

I called my mother the next day and told her what had happened the night before. She said, "Yeah, she is only confirming what I told you already." Later on, I spoke with my mother's best friend, Fran, who told me something I didn't know. She asked me, "Do you remember that day you prayed over your mother," I said, "Yes, that was six months ago." "Well, your mother had not been able to walk for a couple of months because she had been having some issues with her legs. After you prayed for her, she was able to walk again." I said, "Wow, really?!" She said, "Yeah! Really! That's why your mother called you the next day to tell you that." What I could not understand is; why my mother did not tell me that six months ago. The only reason I could think of was that it was in God's timing when He wanted me to know this.

WOMEN'S RETREAT

I was invited to attend a women's retreat; this was an opportunity to let myself go; for once, I seriously needed an outlet. I felt like I was in a desperate situation; I had enough strength to put on a brave front, the enemy had tried to drag me down, and at this point, I was at my lowest of the lowest. I needed this retreat. I was fasting and praying on behalf of my husband, marriage, children, and my family as a whole. When I got to the retreat the first night, I boldly cried out to the people of God and asked for prayer. They did not hesitate to gather around and pray over me. On the last day of the retreat, God gave me a word; He used one of their mothers of the church to tell me that, "God will have your husband going in one direction, and He will have you going in another direction, but eventually, He will bring you two back together. That was one of many spoken words over my life that I recorded in my journal. ***Later in the chapter, you will see how this word comes to fruition.***

When I got home, I began to see my situation differently. My prayer life was changing dramatically. I would spend so much time with God, and I was starting to feel *different.* The Lord was lifting me out of this pit that I was in, which felt like a pit of discouragement where I was not my resilient self and felt *lost.* I hated those feelings; it just wasn't me. I wanted to get back to some type of normalcy. I started going on prayer walks that would take about two hours before returning home. One day, while walking, I talked to God about my situation regarding my husband. As I was having this conversation with God about many other things that surrounded our issues, I asked God, "What am I supposed to do with my husband? What exactly do you want me to do with him?" I heard God say in my Spirit, "Keep praying for him!" I said, in shock, "Keep praying for him? God, I've already been praying for that man! What else is there to pray about?! Am I hearing you right, God? Did you say to keep praying for him? Is that what you are telling me to do?"

I had come to the end of the block and was crossing the street. This street has a large intersection, so there was plenty of space between the cross streets. I was walking at a fast pace; when I got to the middle of the intersection, there was a car proceeding to make a left turn but coming at me within inches of where I was walking. Had I not skipped up just a few steps, I would have been hit and thrown, who knows how many feet away. It was a young lady driving, talking with another young lady in the passenger seat, not paying attention to her surroundings. It was such a close call; I knew right then that this was no coincidence; the enemy was trying to take me out! In fact, I audibly said, "Oh devil!" in bewilderment, "You are trying to take me out!" I began to praise God so hard! Right then, I knew that the enemy was not a happy camper.

But still, I couldn't figure out what he was after. I went right back into my conversation with God. I said, "Well, I guess you do want me to pray for my husband, so what do you want me to pray about?" The Holy Spirit said, "There are some things in his heart that I want out that are connected to his past, and I want him to surrender it all. I want him to surrender his whole heart to me."

Meanwhile, as I continued to receive more instructions from God, the young lady who almost hit me had sincerely taken it upon herself to make a U-turn just to apologize to me. Most people would not have done that at all. Besides, it had been at least a good five minutes or so that went by, and I thought she was long gone by then. It felt like this was just another confirmation that I was on the right path with what God wanted me to do.

It was now apparent that my strength in the Lord was something I was not cognitive of. Think about it, my brother or sister, why would God ask me to stand in the gap for my husband? You really have to be in tune with God to follow the instructions that He gives you. Rather than falling out and crying about things that weren't going right, God allowed me to see what my husband could not see for himself in the spirit. I also had my moments; we were both unaware of some things. Remember, I, too, had no clue what was going on and was asking God constantly why are were having all these issues? I couldn't even tell you when they started or how to resolve them. I still had no clue how long we would go through this turbulence or what I used to call the ***"Twilight Zone"*** charade.

I asked God, "Why am I going through all of this drama?" Just then, the Lord reminded me of a prayer that I had prayed years ago when I was single. I understood that marriages did not always work out, and I did not want to go through that a second time. I promised God that if He gave me another chance to get married again, I would come to Him first for every problem we might have instead of walking away. I would come to Him first for His help in making decisions to fix any problem.

Through speaking with a good friend, God reminded me of this Scripture in **Numbers 30:2**, which says, "If a man vow (pledges) a vow unto the LORD or swear an oath to bind his soul (commit himself) with a bond; he shall not break his word, he shall do according to all that proceedeth out of his mouth." When I realized that it was a serious vow I had made to God, I felt conflicted. It was also in that moment that God reminded me that He loves His son, He has a purpose for him and us, and that He chose me to be that helpmate that will continue to stand in the gap for him, again, this was not a surprise to God. Still, it sure was a surprise to me because I would tell myself, "This can't be real; life just cannot be like this every single day." I believe there is no question of my husband's love for God, but to be honest, the things that took place caused me to scratch my head and wonder. It took me some time to process all of this. Eventually, I surrendered and kept pressing forward.

CHAPTER EIGHT

Behind The Scenes

While going through these various challenges, the Lord would speak to me many times weekly and sometimes daily. It was as if He was coaching me through this hard time. The Lord put it in my heart to do an absolute fast for three days one day. I was so desperate for my family that I obeyed without hesitation. Now, I had done a three-day fast before, but with water. I would be doing a fast with no food or water this time. It was God's true fast for me during this time. I needed an answer from God, and soon! I prepared myself mentally, spiritually, emotionally, and physically.

Mentally, because I was about to go without food and water, and who would do something like that? A person who is serious and desperate for God to do something would!

Spiritually, because this would be my time to know God in a way, I had never known Him before.

Emotionally, because my dependence on God was all I had at the moment. He was my only source of comfort at that time, and finally…

Physically, because I needed some help getting on that floor, I was determined to lay down prostrate before Him until I received an answer.

I grabbed some pillows to tuck under my chest area and a blanket because it was cold, and I needed something that was going to keep me warm while I was on the floor for however long I was going to be down there. I'm just keeping it real for you guys! I meant business!

On the first day of the fast, I woke up early and dropped the kids off at school. My husband had already left for work. Now it was just me and God alone. I said to God, "You know I can't sing, but I am going to sing this song to You anyway." I started to sing this song that we used to sing when I was in the youth choir. It came from the scripture **Proverb 3:5-6,** which says, "Trust in the Lord, with all thine heart; and lean not unto thine own understanding. In all thy ways, acknowledge Him, and He shall direct thy paths." When I finished singing that song, it was as if a light bulb had switched on; I said, "Oh, God!! You're saying trust You!" He was letting me know that He knows what I need.

The second day, I went back to our family room and laid myself prostrate before the Lord. This time, I heard God say, "I will take care of your family." The third day, I went back again and laid myself prostrate before the Lord and just praised His Name for the peace I needed from Him and to let me know that He would be there for my family and I.

I was so excited because I knew that God was doing some amazing things through me, and I wanted to share them with my husband, but God stopped me in my tracks as I was standing in the doorway of my kitchen. I heard God say, "Your whole household is anointed. I have something for you too, but you cannot tell your husband yet, for he is not ready to receive or accept you. I am still working on you; this cannot be revealed until you understand who you are first and you have received and accepted what I have put inside of you."

Then, I saw a vision; it was displaying different scenes. We were in our church; I saw my husband standing at the pulpit; he was sobbing with his head bent over while our oldest son was ministering in song. You see, my brother or sister, the difference here is, there have been many Sundays that my son would sing at this exact location by the piano, but my husband never stood at the pulpit at the same time while he was singing. Years later, this same scene would come to fruition and why it was so significant to us.

Within that same week, following my fast, we were all chilling at home; I went into the living room to do something, when out of the blue, my oldest son tells me, jokingly, "Hey, mom! Dad and I were watching TV, and I was trying to read a word on the bottom of the screen." He laughed and said, "Dad says that I need some glasses." Right then, an alarm went off in my mind. Some weeks before that day, I had gotten a letter from his school stating that they had given him an eye exam, and they felt that he needed to see an optometrist. Now, I don't know how I missed this, but for some reason, I felt that what my son was saying was not a joke. I asked him a couple of questions and decided to make him an appointment to see the eye doctor.

Later in the week, he had his eyes examined, and sure enough, he was going to need to wear glasses. It was God that gave me the answer that I needed. Knowing this gave me more clarity as to why my son's behavior in school was weird and may have contributed to why he was doing some crazy stuff in school. No, I am not excusing a lot of what he had done but getting glasses did help. It was one of the best answers that I had received from God! When my son entered the eighth grade, I wasn't receiving as many calls from his school as before. I was so relieved! It was these things that had put a lot of pressure on me!

One Sunday morning, my son and I visited my friends' church. It just so happened that the same visiting Evangelist who spoke into my life the last time now had a word for my son. It came time to collect the tithes and offering, and when she saw my son, she walked over to where we were standing. As she was in the spirit, she prayed that he'd be shielded from any stray bullets. She told him that he was smart but he didn't want anyone to know how smart he really was. She told him that the decisions he made would affect those around him. She also said that in the next twelve years, the Lord will be using you; everything you say, every decision you make, will be to help other young men in society."

When the Evangelist spoke these things over my son, what had not been clear to me before had now become crystal clear. But, by this time, a lot of damage had been done, and it caused a significant amount of anger, resentment, bitterness, and strife in our household. It looked as if we were never going to be over this *madness.*

It came time for my husband to be ordained as the Minister of our church. I was at a place where I was seeking God's face like never before. Although I had been in my home church since I was a little girl, I was so uncomfortable in that moment and it felt as if God had me isolated. I've now come to understand that God was transitioning me from a little girl to a young woman of God. It felt so strange; it was as if the people that knew me as a little girl could not or did not want to see the young lady that God was transforming from the inside out.

Kindly understand me, my brother or sister, in my mind, I was here to support this man of God, who is my husband, but for whatever reason, it did not look like that from others' point of view. I felt so out of place, and all I kept asking myself was, "Why?" I'd been here my whole life, and there was no reason I should feel uncomfortable in my own home church, right? I still didn't know where the root of all this tension was coming from. I was simply waiting for this whole thing to unfold. I felt as if I was sitting in front of a television screen watching a new movie while waiting for the next scene to come on so I could find out what happens next.

CHAPTER NINE

The Fast That Gave Me Insight To Continue To Stand

It was now the beginning of the year; I had plans to see a play that someone was having at their church; as I got on the freeway, my sister called me and asked what I was doing? I told her where I was heading, and she asked if I could pull over. At that moment, I knew something was wrong, so I tried to remain calm and got off the freeway. My sister had been sick and was in the hospital, so I was not expecting her to tell me what she needed to say to me. When I told her that I was parked, she spilled out that my older sister had died earlier that day. I was in a state of shock; I could not believe my ears. I remained quiet as she told me some of what she knew because she didn't have all of the details as to what caused her death. Knowing that she was in the hospital, I asked her if she was okay. My sisters were close, and at the same time, they were also in a weird way, at odds with one another, but you could tell that they loved one another. I was sure that this news did not sit well with her. As my sister continued to express her feelings about this, all I could think about was the last phone call I'd gotten from her. She would always ramble on and on about how I was her baby and go down memory lane about me as an infant and child and what she did for me. Out of that conversation, I could hear, "I loooovvvve you, baby," like twenty times over the phone. I would be hurting for a while, knowing that she was gone. One thing that has brought me comfort over the years is understanding that it must have been their time to go. I know that God has His own timing when it comes to these kinds of things, but there are times when hints of sadness come over my heart, and it hits me harder on certain days versus others because I knew that she genuinely loved me. I sometimes want to call her just to hear her voice again, *but now, I can't.* Unfortunately, I could not make it to her funeral, but I was able to write a loving note in her obituary. Maybe it was not meant for me to attend during that time, and I say this because the following year, there would be another strike that I would have to bear.

Over time, the decision was made to make my husband the Senior Pastor of our church, and he was now being installed. It never occurred to me that something like this would ever take place in my life. Being the wife of a Pastor was not something I would have planned for myself. Not only that but the pastor of the very same church that I grew up in! "My Safe Haven." I learned many things during this process, and one was that the enemy was not going to stop planting bad seeds or fighting us just because we said yes to God. If anything, the enemy stepped it up a notch!! I soon realized that I had a fight on my hands that I was not quite prepared for, so I too had to roll up my sleeves and take things up a notch with the **power of God by my side and on the inside of me!!**

Although I always intended to support my husband, I now understand that the enemy set all kinds of traps for us to fail way before we knew the call on our lives. Of all the years that I had been at my home church, this had to be one of the most uncomfortable events I have ever attended. There was so much confusion and division among the members, and the funny thing is, I couldn't understand where it was coming from. Some were in favor of my husband becoming senior pastor, but those who were skeptical voiced their opinion as to why they weren't in agreement with the decision. It also felt like my husband (as an individual), our marriage, and our family was being monitored.

I really didn't know how to react to all of the confusion, so I continued to sit there and watch what was displayed before me. I was outside looking in, and I could see how the enemy was literally using some as puppets. Some were being used to gossip and slander others, while some simply made it clear through their expressions that they could not stand their brother or sister. I didn't fully understand why so much warfare was directed towards me. Let me pause right here and tell you this, my brother or sister, God will send people your way to pray you through difficult times and not just anyone, but ones with the right spirit. He will send people who honestly believe in Him, you, and loves the Lord. What I had to endure was no easy thing, not by a long shot. There were many times I've wanted to retaliate or just simply let it all go and walk away. It was days like those when it felt like God would take me by my collar, pull me back and say, "NO! Don't do it! You will mess up My plans! What does My Word say?" My bewilderment would be at its best, and in the midst of my pain, I would remember a scripture. One which says, "…Vengeance is Mine; I will repay, saith the Lord," **Romans 12:19, KJV** I had to learn not to give place to the devil like I had done on many occasions.

I had to learn to live peaceably with all men. Now, was that easy…? **NOPE**! I think God was testing me; it was a battle between my flesh and the spirit. I didn't like what was happening around me, and I questioned how long things would be the way it was. There was always a big ole' '*elephant*' in the room. I asked God what the point of going through all this was? What was most weird about being in this place is, I felt that I had been here before; it was like I was in this state of confusion trying to figure out what I had done in my life to feel like it's been flipped upside down, instead of right side up. It felt like I knew what I was supposed to do (pray) while going through this chaos, but it was frustrating because it seemed as if I was the only one seeing the truth of what was taking place. I could see what the enemy was trying to accomplish, and it looked like he was winning.

I also saw a different personality in my husband, and it was becoming increasingly harder to deal with. I couldn't pinpoint precisely when things had changed; I just knew I had to keep my focus on Jesus. Here is what I had to keep in mind, if I took care of God's business, He would take care of mine. The enemy was busy throwing fiery darts at me, and I was doing my best to duck and dodge them. I was truly in the midst of warfare! Lol. No, it wasn't funny at that time, but when I actually sat down and put it all together, knowing that I have the victory and that the enemy will lose was now pleasing, and I could now watch how my story would unfold unto the glory of God! Understand me, my brother or sister, this is my testimony of what was happening to me; not knowing all of the struggles that my husband was experiencing on his end, he has his own story to tell. There was a time when the enemy would attack me through something that was said so boldly, knowing that I would be hurt or annoyed by these things, but God would always do something amazing to change my focus so I would have the mind to pray still and minister to someone else.

As I was approaching forty, I had made up in my mind that I wanted to celebrate my birthday at the church since my life reflected and revolved around it. I began to inquire about having a celebration. I wanted a reunion with most of the young adult choir coming together to sing some of our best and old songs that we used to sing. It would be a time to fellowship like old times. I wanted to celebrate this time because this was where I met my Heavenly Father and the people whom I love dearly; I wanted them to celebrate with me. While the enemy tried to create an issue through others regarding me celebrating in my home church, God did something for me one night that no one would have ever understood. This was one of those nights that God Spoke to me. He told me to "**Stand**." All that week, I kept hearing in my Spirit to **Stand**. One of the groups that came to celebrate with me sang a song called *'STAND'* by Donnie McClurkin. It was a young man that was singing in the background who took part in the lead; in the midst of him singing, he gave his testimony, and in the process, he said to me, "I don't know who you are, I have never met you before, but from what everyone has been saying about you, you keep on doing what you are doing!" Those words were just what I needed as all that week; the Lord kept telling me, "Keep **STANDING**, I've got you!".

Later that week, following my birthday celebration, I kept having unsettling feelings in my spirit. You might call it spiritual discernment. It was as if I was preparing for something, but what? My brother or sister, let me pause right here; a few months prior, I went on a twenty-one-day fast on behalf of my marriage and family. Of course, no one knew what I was doing. I was in a place where I could see the enemy's tricks and schemes, and the only way to fight this was through fasting and prayer. This was my only weapon; this was my only hope. You see, this was not just about the marriage itself; it was about me going before the Lord to help me conduct myself as God's child, as His servant, and as a wife. We had an adversary running rampant, and I needed

God to show me where the root was coming from! Some days, I did not eat at all, some days, I would just have water, and then, other days, I would eat one meal within the guidelines of what I was led to have. A few months later, after I finished the fast, I realized that God had prepared me for this day.

So, now, we are back to the week I had this unsettling feeling in my spirit. I was getting ready to lay my head down; just before my head hit the pillow, I heard the Spirit say, "Go look at one of the old cell phones on your dresser." I was kind of perplexed and sleepy, and I asked, "Go look at the phone?" There was an old cell phone that was no longer in service, but my younger son was able to play games on them; I was thinking and saying out loud, "I'm not going to do that!" I laid my head down on the pillow and went to sleep. It was 7 a.m. when I opened my eyes, and I heard the Spirit say, "*GO LOOK AT THE PHONE!*" So, I went to get the phone; I opened it up and said, "Now, what am I looking at?" Well, I tell you that the Holy Spirit was very specific.

I saw communication back and forth between my husband and a family member regarding my oldest son and I. It was incredibly shocking and honestly very judgmental, critical, and negative. You would have to be a person who detests the ground that person walks on to say the things in that text. What I saw was an open display of words from someone who secretly despised me but told me they loved me to my face. What I witnessed was **years** of intentional toxic communication. I was beyond hurt by what I saw and read; I can only describe it as a betrayal. Thank God for the people who prayed me through during that difficult time. I did not give the specifics, but they kept me lifted anyhow. It was nothing but the Grace of God that got me through that rough patch. What I saw on the phone caused me to get up and stumble as I was walking into my living room. I had to take my oldest son to school, and I did everything in my power not to let him see me break down and cry. I remember staggering and feeling as if I was drunk. I felt so dizzy it took my breath away. All I could muster from my mouth was, "**JESUS**.... **JESUS**.... **HELP ME**!" I opened up the bathroom door while my husband was in there preparing for work, and I looked at him and said, "Now, I know!"

My husband looked at me in amazement as if he were saying, "*WHAT*?!" I just closed the door and hurried to get my son to school. I was so upset; he could tell that something was wrong. He kept asking me, "Mom! What's wrong?" As a mother, you try to defend your kids from people on the outside, especially when you know they may not be a great influence on them, but there is nothing more devastating than having to protect them from those close to you. As soon as my son got out of the car, tears started flowing down my face. When I got back home, all I could do was wait in the driveway until my husband left for work. I have endured so much throughout my entire life, maybe not like others who have possibly gone through worse than I have, but this was so heartbreaking to experience. This thing shook me to my core and hit me smack dab in my heart! I began to seek God in prayer and asked Him to help me but what happened next surprised me.

As I was crying and carrying on, the Lord reminded me about the fast I had done months ago, and questions began to form in my mind. Questions like, why do you think this is happening now? Why do you think God allowed you to see what you saw? What do you think He wants you to do with that information? So, I had to gather myself and begin to analyze the situation. Some of the pieces started to come together. The Lord gave me answers and allowed me to see exactly what was going on. Finally, everything was making sense to me now. The Lord also showed me that a powerful testimony would come out of this situation. He gave me a little glimpse of the victory that was to take place. I didn't know how He would do it, especially since what I was looking at in front of me looked like an impossible circumstance. When you serve a God that makes ways out of no way, you have no choice but to say, "Okay, Lord, I trust You. I know you can fix this. I just need Your strength to help me get past this because if You don't help me, we will not make it!"

Even after I figured out the piece of the puzzle, I was still upset about the entire situation because it revealed a lot of what had taken place, what was happening, and why. I was beginning to see why the enemy tried to take me out and why he did not want me to stand in the gap for my husband. I was also beginning to see how the enemy was using these messages to challenge my confidence in God, my relationship with Him, and the anointing He has placed upon my life. Through years of lies and manipulation, the enemy was trying to separate our family. Some of us know that Satan will use every tactic to destroy anything that will bring God glory, but we tend to become slack in being watchful; we become slack in using our weapon of prayer over our spouses, children, home, and ourselves. We aren't watchful because we know that we wouldn't do anything to harm our family, not realizing there's an enemy seeking to devour us.

Suppose a family is not praying together as one unit. In that case, someone must take the initiative to pray over their family and themselves, especially when you see that there is bondage. When there is no communication, nothing will get resolved, and there will be a continuous cycle of dysfunction; issues will pile up one on top of the other until you finally get to the core issue of your problem. It's hard to keep up with all of this alone; that's why God wants us to be a team and do things according to His Word.

It took a really good spiritual friend that believed in the power of God to pray for me through this situation. My spirit had become very weak; I was losing my strength to fight this thing. I wrestled with this situation for a minute because I had also found out more hurtful things that just make you want to forget about your relationship with God and do damage control on folks! I told you all I am being honest and transparent. Yes, the Lord had given me the answer to what I prayed, but I didn't think I had enough strength to handle it. This pain of betrayal, along with everything else, was becoming lodged deeply in my heart, and I could feel the heaviness in my chest. When I tried to breathe, the weight of the pain would be there, and it wasn't lifting. For several days, I would have flashbacks of the messages; they would replay in my mind repeatedly. I had to take those thoughts captive and rebuke the enemy constantly.

It was like the enemy was laughing and tempting me to do what any other person would have done when they wanted to get back at someone. Instead, those prayers those God sent to keep me lifted during this time were somehow working on me. About three days later, the Lord put it in my heart to forgive, and I knew that I did not have a choice; besides, I didn't feel like walking around with a bitter and resentful heart. I think that would have been harder to bear than what was revealed. When you're tenderhearted, you dare to love deeply, and I have come to realize that when you love deeply, you hurt deeply. I left myself open to this pain and realized that I would only be holding on to proof of my pain if I continued feeling this way.

If I continued with these feelings, I would try to protect myself in a way that would not necessarily be pleasing to God, and my trust in Him would have gone completely out of the window.

If I had walked around with a wounded heart, it would have caused me to retaliate in defense of being deeply hurt, and I did not want to be held captive by those feelings. So, I had to fight with my flesh and plead with God to help me, and when I finally said the words, "I forgive you," to my husband, I meant it. Those words needed to come out of my mouth, and once I spoke those words, the pain was *lifted from my chest*, and I was able to breathe again! Hallelujah!

Although it did not take me long to forgive, the words I saw continued popping up in my mind; it took a while for the memory of it to be forgotten. While I was in the midst of this trial, it was the Word of God that helped me to understand that the devil wants to torment us into thinking that he has the upper hand. Still, God said, "Wherefore take unto you the whole armor of God, that ye may be able to withstand in the evil day and having done all, to stand" **Ephesians 6:13, KJV**. I still had to work through the process of healing. I had to remind myself that I must forgive even if no one else acknowledged what they did, swept it under the rug, or acted as if nothing happened. I still had to forgive *daily*.

Naturally, there still has to be some form of boundaries, even when it comes to those close to you. This required me to get out of my flesh and yield to the fact of what God had already done for me through Jesus; as God's forgiveness flowed to me, I needed to lean in, cooperate with it, and let God's forgiveness flow through me to other people. My brother or my sister, this is what God has already done for every one of us. It wasn't based on my feelings, which is why God tells us not to keep a record of wrongs. This is why the enemy fights with us so much when it comes to our feelings. I don't have to own other people's mistakes and make it my fault that these things have taken place.

I believe the Lord wanted me to learn to have faith and trust in Him. Although I endured hurt, I can now have compassion for someone who's broken and hasn't healed from their past. When you hurt people, it's because you've been hurt yourself. Hurt comes from an experience with hurt, so when they hurt you, it does not come from them having a desire to hurt you; it comes from acting out from their unhealed pain. Just because the deed was done to you does not mean that it's *because* of you. In asking God why this was happening to me, I was reminded that Jesus was persecuted. He was hated on, spat on, and lied on. He gave me a glimpse of how He felt when He suffered for our sake. He knew what the bigger picture would look like to those that would finally come to the knowledge of His Sovereignty, His Lordship, and His Deity. He suffered for us, and yet, He loved us so much so that He let those very people that falsely accused Him nail him to the cross, and while He was up there, He Said, "Father forgive them for they know not what they do…" **Luke 23:34, KJV**

My God, this made me love Jesus that much more, and in turn, it helped me learn to love my husband that much more and understand that what I was dealing with was bigger than us! It became a little easier for me to forgive, and you can imagine that the enemy did not like that at all. Just when I'd regain my strength in the Lord, the enemy would try and snatch the Word away from me by throwing more fiery darts. The memory of what was said, who said it, and all sorts of things he was behind made me want to give up and throw in the towel. I almost had a hard time trusting again. I had to pray my way through but thanks be to God, He also had others praying me through continuously. God said in **Matthew 11:28,** "Come unto me all ye that labor and are heavy laden, and I will give you rest." With God's help, I kept pressing my way through.

CHAPTER TEN

Losing My Sister, But Still Standing

Not long after what was revealed through the phone conversations, I was at Sunday morning service and spoke with a lady who has been a part of my family my whole life. My sister had referred to her as her mother. She expressed that my sister had been in the hospital and was not doing too well. I was surprised at my sister because usually, she would call and tell me if she had been admitted or not. My sister had been sick for a long while, and although she was a fighter, I was still overly concerned for her. When I got home, I found out more details concerning my sisters' condition, and I made arrangements to see her. She lived about three to five hours away, so I drove straight through without stopping. I just didn't know what to make of the situation. It was late that Friday night when I arrived. Her friend had been taking care of her while she was asleep. I told her to go home and try to get some rest, that I would watch over her. I slept in the recliner that the room provided. A couple of hours later, I thought I heard my sister's friend come back to the hospital to continue to watch over my sister. I watched her care for my sister with love and compassion. I was glad somebody was able to take care of her when I wasn't able to.

"But my God shall supply all your needs…" **(Philippians 4:19, KJV)**

It was now Saturday morning, and when my sister woke up, she was so happy to see her little sister! We chit-chatted a little before she dozed back off to sleep. Her friend and I had spent time speaking with doctors about her tests and medications, what was and wasn't working. They decided to downgrade her from ICU to a telemetry floor, but she had to go back up to ICU in the midst of them transporting her. It was an up-and-downhill battle. Later that day, the Lord put it on my heart to ask my sister that hard question. You know, the question that *nobody* wants to ask? I sat down next to her on the bed, lovingly rubbing her hair as I asked her, what do you want us to do if something happens to you? So, she gave me and her best friend instructions on what to do.

The next day, it was time for me to get back home. As I was preparing to leave, my sister was resting; I kissed her and told her that I loved her. Her play sister and I touched and agreed in prayer over her. I didn't even want to entertain the thought that this would be the last time I saw her. I was kind of numb on the inside, and I didn't want to deal with it at that moment. I did my best to be strong. I walked out of the hospital to my car with tears running down my cheeks, thinking to myself, *here we go again!* I know that God has His own timing, but I just couldn't get a grip on that one.

As I was driving home, I felt more tears pouring down my cheeks; I wanted to beg God not to take my sister, I wanted to believe that she would be miraculously healed and would be able to go back home like she always did. I just did not want to believe that if she left, I would not have anybody to love me the way she loved me or be as close to anyone as she and I were. Somehow, I just knew that things would be different with all of the difficulties she was facing; you could tell that she was tired, really tired. It was too much for me to bear; I tried to stop thinking about it and numb my thoughts, but the pieces of my heart were just breaking the farther I was driving away from her. I said to the Lord, God, I need you so much, please give me strength!

I got that dreadful call about three weeks into that New Year after my fortieth birthday. My sisters' friend told me that my sister was gone. At that moment, I felt that I needed to let my heart (how I felt) take a back seat for a moment. I had to focus on what my sister had requested us to do for her. My sister's best friends and I put our heads together to get things done. My sister wanted my husband to do her eulogy and wanted her older nephew, my son, to sing. Her best friends made the arrangements on their end to get her body cremated and transport it safely to our destination while I was able to take care of things on my end. My church family did a tremendous job of making sure everything flowed the way it was supposed to. I thanked God for their support, but there's nothing worse than not having the support of your spouse, especially at a time like this. I say this because I felt I was left to grieve on my own through the process and him not staying by my side for the repass was hurtful to me. Oh, the enemy had his foot in our home big time, but I had to keep pressing my way through! My sister loved her brother-in-law, she had always spoken very highly of him, and I was not going to taint her view of him because what she had spoken was the truth. We just had some demons we were fighting that wanted to get in the way of the truth.

Both my big sisters had passed precisely one year and eight days apart. The one that just passed was the one I was really close to. Her love almost outshined my other oldest sister, but it was all in love. In my first book, "My Safe Haven," I already shared how much they both adored me, but this sister took the cake.

We spoke weekly, and she adored her nephews so much. Here is a very transparent moment, my brother or sister. Even though I had let some of my grief out at my sister's homegoing, there was still a lot more to release. I couldn't wrap my mind around why the main people I knew genuinely loved me the most had to leave me here with those who did just the opposite? That part right there was mind-boggling to me. I wasn't blaming God; I just did not understand why He did not at least allow one of them to stay here. I wasn't trying to be selfish, but it got to the point where things just seemed so unbearable to deal with, and I felt so alone. This one right here, I needed to depend on God to the tenth power! I needed Him so badly. It had only been five years since my sister's passing, and sometimes, I think I am still grieving over one or the other or both at the same time.

It still hits me at different times; one evening, in particular, I hit a rough patch thinking of my sisters. This is what happens when you are alone a lot, and if you don't keep your mind occupied with something positive, your mind will wander. I began to question God again as I felt the pain of missing my sisters so deeply. As I was lying down in my room, I said, "God, my sisters are gone; why does it feel like there is a deeper hole forming in my heart? Why did you have to take them away right now, at a time when I am going through this heartache here at home? Can't you see that this is too much? Can't you see that I am hanging by a thread? God, I know that you may think that I can bear this, but right now, Father, I just don't know if I can take it anymore; you are going to have to give me a break from this; I need you to please space these trying times that I am having. Right now, I can't even see that; this too shall pass because it seems like there won't be anyone else to love me the way that my sisters loved me. God! I am seriously having a hard time down here. It seems as if I am being faced with the hardest challenges of my life, dealing with people who just don't have the capacity to sincerely know and love me back. As a matter of fact, how about just being sincerely kind? That would be nice too." At that very moment, I could feel God wrapping his arms around me, rocking me until I fell asleep. Sometimes, you just need a good cry so that you can release the pressures of this world. Remember, weeping may endure for a night, but joy comes in the morning. **(Psalm 30:5, KJV)**. I was able to get up the following day feeling stronger than I did the day before and decided to try it one more time, knowing that God will never leave me in this thing all by myself.

We weren't able to locate my last sister. It had been many years since I last saw her. At that time, she did not know about either one of them passing. It would be about a year later when a family member spotted her and told her about their passing. Of course, she was shocked. I still have not spoken with her. I pray that God will bring us together according to His Will and His Time one day.

"To everything, there is a season, and a time to every purpose under the heaven:" **Ecclesiastes 3:1, KJV**

After all that transpired, this would be the year the Lord revealed many things to me. I visited a church where the same Evangelist who had given me a Word the first time would be preaching again. It happened to be on her birthday. As she finished her sermon, she called me and my youngest son up to the altar. She saw something in the spirit---she stated that there was a spirit of anger upon him, but she did not know where it was coming from. She said the enemy was fighting him, so she prayed against the spirit. She also spoke to me and said, "You talk faith outside of the home, but when you get home, it becomes a whole different story because you are faced with many challenges." She said, "You have control over your children, but there are things that are surrounding you that you cannot control; you are to let God control and deal with that. Your lives are going to change like never before."

The next month I attended a retreat, and the Lord Spoke through another anointed Evangelist; she was in the midst of preaching when she called me up, took my hand, twirled me around like I was Cinderella, and began to sing the chorus to a song by **VaShawn Mitchell** saying "*It's turning around for me.*" As she was singing, I felt this lovely sensation come over me. Imagine that old fabric softener commercial that used to come on TV; they had a big brown teddy bear on the screen telling the viewers how soft their blanket was. While the blanket would be floating up in the air, the teddy bear would fall onto the soft fabric with such confidence and delight; this blanket had enough strength to hold the teddy bear as he was floating into the air. That's the best way I could describe what I felt that night. I ended up on the floor for a little while, but when I got up, man! I felt so light. I don't think I've ever felt that way before. *It was so awesome.* There were so many things that happened this particular year; I had no choice but to stay focused. God had given me so many instructions for handling certain situations whenever they were to occur in the future that I had to write everything down to keep up with them. God let me know that He would deal with my situation, and He kept telling me to "Stand."

My position was to stand and continue to watch God do things that amazed me, along with thanking and praising Him for keeping me, no matter how it looked to other people. I had to **Stand** while being left out of decisions I should be involved in as a wife and mother. I had to **Stand** in the gap, not only for my own family but also for others. I had to **Stand** in the midst of every situation and circumstance I was facing, no matter what it looked like. I had to continuously remind myself that the Lord was taking care of my business!

CHAPTER ELEVEN

Isolated Behind The Scenes

It had been three years since the falling out I had with my family when my oldest son stayed with my mama and grandmother. I was now at a place where I was ready to come around my family again, but I did develop some hurtful feelings while I was missing in action. I remember praying and asking God to help me get to a place where I could feel comfortable spending time with them again. I had to deal with the pain that I felt in my own home, but the hurt and disappointment from my other family was something I could not deal with at the same time. I would ask God to let me deal with them another day, another time. It was too much to take on all at once. I didn't have the time or the energy to prove my self-worth to anyone, only God. It was too hard to prove anything to anyone who was not walking in the right Spirit. There were two things that I asked of God; one was that my relationship with Mama be restored, that He would allow me to actually sit down and talk with her one on one so that we could talk out our differences without any interference. I had not spoken with my grandmother, so I didn't realize that she was hurt, nor did I understand the reason for how she felt. A few years later, based on the conversation I had with my grandmother, I was able to put two and two together and figure out what kind of trick the enemy had tried to play on the both of us. The enemy almost succeeded in destroying my relationship with my mama and grandmother behind one issue in particular. The same family member the Lord exposed through having me read messages on the phone had also gotten into the ears of my aunt, mama, and grandmother.

Despite all that had transpired, I believe God was dealing with me about forgiveness. Forgiveness is such a hard word to deal with, especially when you have to forgive multiple people at once. Do you think trying to forgive one person is hard? Try forgiving several. You see, my brother or sister, I didn't have any problems shutting down and separating myself from those I felt had done something to me, and, in turn, they may have thought that I'd done them wrong. My issue was with ***letting it go*** because not one person asked me what happened? Some may have felt they already knew the answer based on what someone else said to them, and what they heard made sense to them. Still, no one had heard my side. I want to add that although nobody asked me what my side of the story was, I can understand that not everybody wants to hear your problems; most people have issues themselves. The struggle was real! I was in a place where not many involved cared to hear the truth, not my natural family or church family. In fact, there was one person throughout the entire ordeal who asked if I was okay? I believe that some who had doubts about what they heard felt they weren't in a position to ask me anything. Honestly, it's still a mystery of what was said or is happening.

God only allowed certain people in my corner because I believe that He knew they would be praying for me continuously. Now, I prayed for myself and others, but it's nothing like having people you know praying and standing in the gap for you. I thank those who secretly prayed for my strength to be in the Lord and in the Power of His Might! This brings me to the scripture about offense. **Luke 17:1, KJV** states, "Then, said He unto the disciples, it is impossible, but that offense will come: but woe unto him, through whom they come!" A person who causes offense intentionally would be better off thrown into the ocean with a heavy stone tied around their neck, so be careful what you do. Within this same text, Jesus is also speaking with the disciples about forgiving others seventy times seven. This scripture can be overwhelming if you aren't rooted and grounded in the Word and Will of God. Now, I didn't mind forgiving people, but did I have to keep forgiving them that many times and so many of them at the same time?! I can talk about how unfair that seems, but God always brings me back to the Cross. A time may come when you feel as if you have to tackle the enemy to take your mind back, and this is where I was! If he could, Satan would have me in a place ready to do some serious damage to those lying and conspiring around me, but God knows how much I love Him and want to please Him!

One night at a Bible study, we were reading from the book of *Romans*, I'm not sure what chapter or verse we were in, but I felt the Holy Spirit say to me, "Now, it's time." I asked Him, "What do you mean?" Somehow, I knew He meant it was time for me to have that talk with my mama. Sure enough, I went over to her house and knocked on the door. I had a lot of reservations because I didn't know how she would react toward me. When she finally came to the door, she was surprised and happy to see me. The first thing she said was, "Why didn't you use your key?" My response was, "I didn't know how you were going to react, so I just knocked to be on the safe side." With tears in our eyes, we hugged one another and sat down on the sofa. Just as I had requested from God, we were able to sit down and have a heart-to-heart talk with one another, with no one around just she and I.

I will share a small part of our conversation I think might be of importance. My mama expressed to me that while my oldest son was in her home for those few weeks, she would hear parts of our conversations between him and me; she said she never heard me tell him I love you when saying goodnight. She told me that she and her mother would tell each other I love you every night when she was growing up, so that bothered her. I had to really try to get my mama to understand my point of view when it comes to such delicate words. I said to her, "Mama, think back on the many times that we have had phone conversations or any time I visited you. Have you ever heard me tell you I love you first? Any time the words I love you came out was when you would say "I love you" to me, then you would hear me say I love you back." She thought back on this, and she said, "Well, come to think of it, no, I never heard you say that first." I expressed to her every time that she asks me to do something for her, I did it, every time she called, I answered, anything she needed, I made myself available. I also asked her, "Have you ever seen me mistreat my kids? They are well fed and well clothed; they get hugs and kisses from me, along with whatever motherly things that I do for them."

I said "Mama, you have to remember that I didn't grow up in the same household with you, daddy, and my brothers. I come from a different background than you all. I was not told I love you every day before leaving for school or every night before going to bed. Sure, I was told I love you by my *(biological)* mother, but it wasn't on a consistent basis, and to be honest, at the time, the proof really wasn't there. Mama didn't understand she was speaking to someone who'd been mistreated and abused most of their life. It was more important for me to *show* you that I love you because you would believe me when I said it. I told her, "Don't get me wrong; I did tell my son I love him; you just didn't hear it the times the times you may have felt I should say it." Mama finally understood where I was coming from. Reality sunk in, and she said I see what you are saying, and I know you love your children; I never doubted that. We ended our conversation with complete understanding and respect as adult women and mother and daughter.

It was now Father's Day; I remember because I didn't have our children sitting with me. There was a particular message preached that Sunday in the morning service, and the following weeks after, I felt burdened down. Some things were said concerning me that were crushing. These were the times I wish I could have said something to defend myself, but the Lord would not allow me to say anything. It was as if God took me by my collar and zipped my lips, but I was hurt. I got in my car, and as I was driving, I cried out to God, and I asked Him to help me come out of this pit I was in. Mind you; I was still grieving the loss of my sisters, going to work, taking care of my kids, and trying to handle my duties as a wife while all these things were happening. So, when I got home, I changed my clothes and decided to see my mama. When I got there, I was ready to leave within five to ten minutes. I gave my mama and others who welcomed me a hug, kissed them goodbye, and left. I could feel a bit of tension still lingering from the family quarrel we had over my son with some of the other family members, and I didn't have the strength to deal with it at that time. It was nothing new; someone was often upset with me but rarely discussed why they were at odds with me.

As I was driving home, the Holy Spirit led me to take a detour to a cousin's home nearby. I got a chance to be used by God to minister to her. Normally when I visited, this cousin would not be home, and it would be her mother (who we called Ms. Olivia) that I would see most of the time. We sat down and conversed with each other, and she began to express to me some concerns she had with her daughter. As she talked, I felt like it was Deja Vu. I had this same experience with my oldest child. I could tell how stressed she was and pretty much at her wits' end. Like myself, she felt like she was going through all of this alone, but thanks be to God, I could speak with her and let her know that she was not alone. I told her that I understood exactly what she was going through and gave her my testimony about the experiences I had with my oldest son.

When your children don't have a relationship with Jesus for themselves, the enemy can easily gain access to them. Satan will use anyone who allows him to, knowingly or unknowingly, in order to distract God's plans for themselves and for you. As I shared my testimony, my cousin cried the entire time God was speaking to her. I got up and used the blessed oil that I carried with me and prayed over her. The amazing thing about all of this is, she experienced deliverance and breakthrough! By the time I finished praying, she felt so relieved; it was like her eyes had been opened to something new and different. It was unexplainable to her; she could not describe what she was feeling; she just kept saying, "WOW!" She felt so much better, and she gave me this big ole hug. At that moment, I realized that it was a hug that I didn't know I needed. I was in desperate need of the biggest, most lovable, and generous hugs a sister could receive! It was amazing what God did for her and I that day. It made up for being so uncomfortable at church earlier and at my dad's family house. I also realized that I was on assignment, and I felt that God was pleased.

I thought, now this was me! This is what makes me feel good! Watching God's people get set free, I thanked God that He let me experience this moment. I give God all the Glory and Honor! I absolutely could not take credit for anything God did through me that day. I began to understand that God was moving me to the next level of my journey to where He wanted to take me. This made me forget about my issues at home and at church. He directed my attention to His business while He was still taking care of *my* business! I parked my car across the street from her house only to realize my car, which was in a church parking lot, was now locked inside the lot! You know what, I didn't care; I was on cloud ten that night! Thankfully for me, my cousin knew who to contact to open the gate back up; it didn't take long for one of the deacons who was on his way home to turn back around and let me out.

Within the following week, one morning, after dropping my kids off at school, I was hungry and decided to stop by a local restaurant to get myself some breakfast. As I waited to be served, the host who offered me a table was making light conversation with me and said, "It looks like you are just getting off from work." She asked me where I worked; I told her which hospital. She said, "Oh, Wow! My sister works there in the nursery, but she's been off work due to an illness." She began to tell me about all the issues in her life while she was serving me; she actually took a quick break to talk with me. The Lord began to minister to her through me, and I could see her trying to hold back her tears. Surprisingly, she received what God said to her and thanked me, glory to God!

Sunday had rolled around again, and my experience in that service was no different than the last. There was so much going on and being said, but I would be about my Father's business as God would have it! It is custom at our church to hug and tell everyone your goodbyes after service. While this was taking place, a lady beckoned for me to come over to the other side of the church. She asked if I could pray with her elderly mother, who had some type of bladder infection. She had this look in her eyes as if she knew something about me. As she was looking directly at me, she took my hand, placed it on her mother's right side, and I prayed for her. Here is the thing, we were in front of a lot of church members, but as I told you earlier, the Lord was helping me to pray out loud, and I didn't have time to say, "Ummm, can we go to the backroom and pray in private?" I felt I had to be obedient and pray right then and there.

A few days later, this same woman gave me a book called *Jesus Calling*. In the front of the book, she had written a note for me not to allow the devil to divide my husband and I and that the devil is a lie, lie, lie! She also had written that I have the victory, and then, on the back of the note, it said: "Stay together." I just believed that God always found a way to encourage me each time I felt discouraged by the things around me. I was so incredibly grateful to my Heavenly Father, and at that time, I could see clearly that He loved me so much and that He was letting me know that 'He's got me.'

One night at work, God had me and a couple of my friends pray over a twenty-one-year-old young lady who was homeless. My friend, who saw the young lady first, told me that the Lord gave her a word to ask the young lady if she knew God? The young lady began to cry. After speaking with the young lady, my friend called my other co-worker and I to pray over her. Here is the amazing thing about this story. The young lady testified that she had had a dream some months ago, that she saw some ladies in uniform praying over her. She said she knew we would pray for her, so she went into the bathroom before coming into the office where we were waiting, and she washed her hands as a symbol of washing off the dirt of her sins. This was a divine setup by God to perform His Work! May the Blood of Jesus continue to wash over this young lady. I thank God for another opportunity to be obedient to His Word and His Will. We were just God's vessels, His Body, His Hands, His Mouthpiece being used for doing what only He can do through us.

Just thinking about how God is getting ready to raise up yet another generation of people that He has anointed and empowered with His Holy Ghost power is wonderful! He is about to show us things that we have never seen before. We are about to hear things that we have never heard before in the Name of Jesus. These are some of the amazing things that God has been doing. How Awesome, ***How Wonderful, How Glorious God Is!!***

CHAPTER TWELVE

Taking Care Of God's Business

One day, the Lord put it in my spirit to fast until after the prayer meeting that evening as I talked with a friend. I had another friend to fast and stand in agreement with me as well. I couldn't explain what would happen; it was just something on my heart to do. I went to the store and bought some red towels. I remember going to the store, and while standing in front of the towel section, I said, "Okay, Lord, what do you want me to do here?" I was instructed to get one big red towel along with a few small red hand towels. I remember being kind of perplexed because I really thought I was tripping; I had no idea what the purpose of me buying some red towels was or how I looked to others walking around the store asking the Lord these questions. I'm sure it looked like I was talking to myself because no one was around me. As I walked towards the cashier, I was going back and forth with God, but still, I was being obedient at the same time. Later that day, as I prepared to go to the prayer meeting, the Holy Spirit instructed me to anoint the towels with oil. I still had no clue as to what was going to take place when I got there. To be honest, I hoped my husband wasn't going to be there. I thought he was only going to make it for Bible study. However, he showed, and at that point, I didn't have time to deal with feelings of intimidation. I didn't have time to worry about how he would react to me. I didn't have time to worry about what argument would take place when we got home. None of those things mattered because I had to be obedient to the Holy Spirit, and that was that!

It was now or never! Honestly, I didn't want to pray, but God gave me the strength to get up and cover my husband with this big red towel as a covering, representing the Blood of Jesus. I started trembling, but I had no time to fear. I covered him with that big red towel and began to plead the Blood of Jesus over him, and everybody in that room came into agreement with me. There was no denying that the Power of God was there! My friend later shared that she saw an angel hovering over one of the members that was also praying in agreement with fervor as I was standing over my husband praying. My friend said she also saw my husband being lifted up. The presence of God was so thick in that room. I had never done anything like this before to my husband or in front of my husband. It was God who gave me the boldness and courage to do what I did! I would have never considered doing anything like that on my own. I don't know what was going through my husband's mind because we were not in the best place with each other, but I believe God was testing me to see if I would be bold for Him. I would rather be behind the scenes, not out in front, but when the Holy Spirit gives me the unction to do something, it becomes an unsettling feeling until I do what I am told, and after I've done it, I feel as if I am back to my normal self.

One morning, my spiritual mother invited me to a World Day of Prayer Meeting. When we got to the church, the men and women were gathered, split into groups, and given a country to pray over. After we finished praying in groups, we prayed collectively. When the program was over, we prepared ourselves to get lunch in the fellowship hall before we left to go home. As my spiritual mother and I were conversing with another woman *(I happened to be the youngest* in this group of wise women), one of the mothers began to share how the Lord blessed her to come through surgery. She also said the doctors wanted to perform another surgery on both of her legs. As she spoke, she went to sit down, and you could tell that she was in pain. I felt the Holy Spirit prompting me to pray for her right then, but I wasn't for sure.

Just as I was turning to leave, the mother said, "I don't want to go under the knife again, y'all, please pray for me." Just then, before I could stop myself, I made a U-turn and said, "Why don't we pray right now?" I thought to myself, "Man, why did I say that?!!" But it was too late; all six women standing there were ready to touch and agree, I had to go forth with prayer! Everyone gathered around me in a circle; I got down on my knees, laid my hands on the mother's knees, and began praying for her. When I finished praying, I felt something come over me; I felt like I was floating. My spiritual mother witnessed the woman getting up differently from how she sat down. She got up with a quickness! There was no pain on her face. As a testimony, the mother said to everyone, "I feel good, I feel really good!" In my mind, I said to God, "What just happened?" I looked at my spiritual mother and asked her the same question! Lol Besides that, my mind was in a state of awe because I knew this was God's doing!

Sometime later, a couple of my coworkers and I set up a time to visit another coworker who'd been sick. The doctors diagnosed her with some form of cancer and had given her a short time to live. We were all on fire for God and ready to pray for this young lady, but before we could meet at the hospital, the school called and requested that I pick up my oldest son because he had gotten sick, which was weird. After all, he rarely gets sick. Then, about fifteen minutes later, my other coworker also received a call saying that her son needed to be picked up from school as well. I don't believe it was a coincidence that both of our children had to be picked up from school around the same time we were going to *pray* for someone. However, we arranged for the boys to be picked up and cared for, but strange things were happening; it was now an issue with getting to the hospital. The enemy was trying to set traps to prevent us from going to the hospital, and we didn't fully understand why until *after* we visited this young lady.

As I was headed to the hospital, my two coworkers rode together to meet me. They informed me that they had come to a detour because the freeway was blocked off, and they had to exit off the highway and enter another route to get to the hospital. We were all praying when they got back onto the freeway, and then, it seemed as if they were the only car on the road; it was like the angels opened the way for them from there; it was smooth sailing. We finally met up at the hospital. We were so excited because we expected a miracle. We did not know how, but we expected God to move on behalf of this young lady. She and her fiancé had four children; they were all so young. So, by the Grace of God, we took out time and prayed for her. We expected a miracle, but nothing of what *we saw right before our eyes.*

When we entered the room, our coworker was lying in bed with her head tilted to the side; she looked very pale. You could see the fear in her eyes. We could tell that she recognized us but couldn't speak, so we immediately began praying and speaking 'life' into her. Just as we finished praying for her, we saw a miracle happening right before our eyes! Life was coming back into her eyes; the paleness of her skin was leaving, and her original skin color was coming back. One of her hands was tightly closed and balled into a fist, but it was now slowly opening, and she was later able to feed herself again. We felt the presence of God in the room! There was a light in the room that wasn't there when we first walked in, and a smile had formed her face. Let me tell you, my brother or sister; we were all so astonished by what God was doing right before our very eyes! Her nurse came in to attend to her by this time, so it was time for us to leave. However, we did not leave the same way we went in, now the fire in our lives had increased the more!!! One coworker rode home with me so we could later attend Bible Study. I'm telling you, if someone saw us, they would have thought we were high on drugs! Lol, We were high, alright! High on what the Spirit of God had done through us! It was ***His Power*** and ***His miracle*** that was performed! What was more remarkable is the teaching at Bible Study happened to come from the book of John. After Jesus performed a miracle, He told His disciples they would do ***greater works!***

John 14:12-15, KJV says, "Verily, verily, I say unto you, He that believeth on Me, the works that I do shall he do also; and greater works than these shall he do, because I go unto my Father. And whatsoever ye shall ask in My Name that will I do, that the Father may be glorified in the Son. **14** If ye shall ask anything in my name, I will do it.**15** If ye love me, keep my commandments."

So, you can imagine how excited we were as we sat there listening! My coworker who went to Bible Study with me stood up and testified because it was definitely a 'Hallelujah' moment for us! Still, only a few people were excited about what God had done. I mean, the look on some of their faces was like, oh okay, that's good. All the while, I'm thinking to myself, why in the world are only a few excited about this?! God said we would be doing these things; He was confirming His word at that moment! Did they believe what His Word said and what was taught? It wasn't until later that I realized others wouldn't receive what God was doing "in or through me," but these were some of the things that God was doing while I was waiting for my breakthrough!

CHAPTER THIRTEEN

In The Midst Of My Trials

It felt as if I was always on assignment for God and was being trained on the job, so to speak. I was learning, growing, being tested, groomed, shaped, and molded into what God was calling me to be for His Kingdom. I had to keep a Kingdom mindset, no matter what others thought of me. As far as I was concerned, this was my only way of survival. My brother or sister, I'm about to share another powerful experience I had with my Heavenly Father that started the ministry I would later come to know as deliverance. On this day, God showed up and showed out! God did something so mind-blowing that there was just *no way* you could tell me that God isn't real! I experienced God as I had never experienced Him *before*!

I was at home doing my hair, and a friend I grew up with called and asked if she could stop by. Of course, I said yes, and when she arrived, she began telling some things that had taken place in her life. I sat there still doing my hair as she shared how she found herself going down an unexpected path. I started to ask her a few questions. One was, what were her reasons for going down the path she had chosen? She responded by saying that it was pretty much an escape from reality. As we continued to converse, she said she wanted help and didn't know what this "thing" was that she couldn't get rid of it. I told her it was a demonic spirit trying to take hold of her mind, body, will, emotions, and soul. As my friend was talking, I was praying in my spirit, asking God to help me and to help His child! I could see what the enemy was trying to do, and I wasn't going to stand by and watch him destroy one of God's children! She has such a powerful anointing upon her life, and with the help of God, the only thing I could do for her was to take what she was asking to the throne of grace, bombard Heaven on her behalf and ***stand*** *in the gap!*

This friend was actually receiving help through other resources, so I was surprised she shared these things with me. I asked her how bad she wanted help; she said, "Whatever it takes!" I asked if I could have her permission to call a friend of mine to explain the situation so we could touch and agree in prayer. She said, "Yes!" I got my blessed oil and rubbed it on her face and hands while my friend who was on the phone began to pray a powerful prayer. As she ended the prayer, I started to pray, and the Holy Spirit took over me. The fire of the Holy Ghost took over, and the friend I was praying for began to vomit. She tried to catch it with her shirt, but some of it spilled on the floor. I continued to pray while the Lord was doing **His** work on her! She ended up on her knees singing praises unto our Heavenly Father!

She had been set free by the Blood of Jesus!!! I stood there in complete shock while she was still singing praises to God! I said to myself, "God is this what you have been preparing me for?! Is this why the enemy has been after my family?" I had witnessed the power of God once again, and I was so amazed that God trusted me enough to help set a captive free! It reminds me of an old hymn that says, "..what can wash away our sins and make me whole again? Nothing but the BLOOD OF JESUS!!!!" No wonder there had been such a struggle in my household! After all that had transpired over the years, more pieces of the "puzzle" were coming together. I was able to see the big picture and gain an understanding of the battle that was taking place with my family, marriage, and church.

During this time, I had a mentor who really taught me the things of God. She is a strong woman of God who is able to see in the Spirit. She played a huge role in my growth in the Lord. I am so grateful to my Lord; He hears our cries for help! One of the most important things she taught me was how to fast and truly seek God's face through prayer. In fact, she would fast and stand in agreement with me, and for that, I am so very thankful to her! Her love for God showed in her strength and power to overcome any situation she faced.

Years of fasting, praying, and getting in the face of God truly helps you to develop spiritual discipline! Speaking of fasting and praying, it just so happened that I worked a day shift instead of my regular shift, which was at night. I don't remember why, but I believe that nothing happens by coincidence. One of my coworkers was finishing her shift; she worked overnight. When I came in to relieve her, the first thing she said was; I need to talk with you. I thought she would speak with me later, but she said, "No, I need to talk with you now!" I said okay. We went to a back room for some privacy, and she began to explain that she had been having issues with one of her young adult children. She expressed that although they went to church, they didn't have a personal relationship with Jesus. My friend also said that her dog wasn't doing so well. She felt something was wrong, and she needed me to pray over her house. What she didn't know was I had just come off of another twenty-one-day fast, but a couple of days before that, the enemy launched an attack. I was cleaning one of the rooms in our house and I noticed a gift bag that was given to my husband. It was unusual for it to be placed where it was. Let's just say I had woman's intuition so, I examined the gift. Upon examining the gift, I saw that it was from the opposite sex. Although my husband looked at it as an innocent gesture, but I felt the gift was inappropriate.

Now, here's the thing, my brother or sister, if you aren't careful, you will miss what God wants to do in you, for you, and through you. We have to stay in prayer, stay on our post, and stay on our guard. The enemy is very cunning, and he will trip you up if you aren't watchful. I almost missed my assignment; I was only two days from ending my fast when I had this confrontation with my husband. I am being completely honest and very transparent; I struggled with being careful of what to say, how to say it, and when to say it. I was aware of the fast, and I could see that the enemy was trying to distract me; however, it was hard to resist in some moments. This may be surprising to hear, but I actually tore down a closet door in our house to let out my frustrations! After that, I left and got a Frappuccino to calm down; hey, I know it's better ways to handle things, but at that moment, it was the only way to keep me from doing something crazier.

Now back to my coworker, she went home; I sat down at the computer and started working when I heard the Holy Spirit say, "You have to apologize to your husband." I said, "WHAT?!!! Nah, man, I didn't do anything!" He said you would not be able to complete your assignment with that thing in your heart, meaning what was in my mind concerning the discussion we had along with the doubt and fears I had. Oh my God! I wrestled with that one all day! I was upset; I didn't feel that I needed to apologize to my husband; after the hot mess, I discovered, if anything, he was the one who should have apologized to me. But the Holy Spirit said to me, "You are not apologizing for why you had the confrontation, but how you behaved during the confrontation." Man, I was not a happy camper! I needed a Horchata Frappuccino for this one. LOL So, on my off day, I went prayer walking to ask God to help me face my husband to apologize for my behavior. When I got back home, I sat down and asked my husband if he had a minute to talk. I think I sat there for a good five minutes with my tongue stuck to my teeth; I felt like crying because I did not want to do it, but I had to be obedient to the Holy Spirit.

It finally came out of my mouth, and I apologized to my husband for my behavior. I also told him that I'd try not to behave that way again. I don't know what my husband was thinking, but he said okay. I don't know if he believed me, but I do think that he thought I was crazy! Even though I felt foolish, I felt relieved that I had gotten that off my chest and hadn't made it harder for myself. I had no idea that what was about to occur at my coworker's house would reveal why I had to apologize to my husband, and I didn't put that together until afterward. The day came that my friend and I met with that coworker *(I had gotten permission to bring her along);* they had been friends for many years. Little did I know that we were in for more than we expected! This was one of those times when the scripture really manifested itself.

"And we know that all things work together for good to them that love God, to them that are called according to His purpose." **(Romans 8:28, KJV).**

We sat down and spoke with my coworker's daughter, but my friend was the one who was able to minister to her and share her testimony. We could feel the presence of God in the room. Many tears were shed as she began to release a lot of hurt, pain, and guilt. She was even able to apologize to her family. The Lord spoke through me and asked if she wanted to accept the Lord as her personal Savior. The Heavens were rejoicing because she said, "YES!" Hallelujah, Glory be to God! My friend led us into prayer, and I continued the prayer that those demons had to go by the power of God in the name of Jesus! Prayers went forth for my coworker, her mother, sister, son, niece, and then her dog. We could feel the weight of the presence of God in that room. It was amazing what took place! In the midst of this happening, God restored the friendship between the friend I brought to pray and the coworker we prayed for. Their friendship was no longer of the world; they saw the spiritual connection. God gave them an understanding of why their friendship had been stagnant. Now the Lord was bringing them back together for such a time as this!

These are the things that took place over the years. I still had to endure the trials at home; I attended church, worked, took care of my kids, cooked, and cleaned up the house. I knew it would only be a matter of time before something would break! Things were still hard to deal with. Actually, they were getting worse, but you know what they say, 'Things get worse before they get better.' I thought of the scripture in Ecclesiastes 9:11 that says, "I returned, and saw under the sun, that the race is not to the swift, nor the battle to the strong, neither yet bread to the wise, nor yet riches to men of understanding, nor yet favor to men of skill; but time and chance happeneth to them all." I had to continue to trust in the Lord.

"I will lift up mine eyes unto the hills, from whence cometh my help. My help cometh from the LORD, which made Heaven and Earth. He will not suffer thy foot to be moved: He that keepeth thee will not slumber."—**Psalms 121:1-3, KJV.**

God kept me busy, so I wouldn't go down a road that led to destruction. Another coworker wanted to speak with me one day while on my lunch break, and we hadn't seen each other in about two months. We went to a private room, and she began to tell me about a situation that she was having at home. She expressed that her significant other's sister had lived with them for a few months but had passed away unexpectedly. She said she now felt uncomfortable in her home and felt a dark presence. She asked if I would come to her house to pray over it because she didn't know anyone who was more spiritual or honest enough to get a prayer through. She felt that I had a connection with God that nobody else had in her eyes. As she told me this, I felt so humbled, and I said to her, "You do know I believe in the name of Jesus?" I asked her this because she believed in God and the universe. I needed her to understand that it was God who would do what she was asking. She said, "Yes, that's why I'm asking you because I believe you have a connection with God and can reach Him."

"I am Alpha and Omega, the beginning and the ending, saith the Lord, which is, and which was, and which is to come, the Almighty." **Revelation 1:8, KJV**

I often asked for permission to include my friend to pray with me; she said yes; she was also a very good friend of hers. We set up a date and time to meet at our friend's house. Once again, the power of God showed up with so much force, which made those demonic forces leave her house! The following Friday, my friend called me and said, "I don't think you realize how anointed you are! She said the heaviness she felt was now lifted, and she could 'breathe' again." All I could do was thank God for what He had done once again. God and His Power, the Almighty One, the All-Knowing One, had done it again! Glory be to God!!!

I love Him so much!

I believe the enemy was really upset with me at this point. I went prayer walking a couple of days after meeting with my friend; I had my earphones in my ear listening to a gospel song, when all of a sudden, out of the left side of my peripheral, I saw something coming at me from across the street which was huge and long. By the time I looked up, a giant black dog that looked like a wolf was charging towards me! He came at me so quickly that I fell on my backside and lifted my foot against his face because that's how close he was to me, the dog, and I was eye to eye. I will never forget his evil red eyes and how he was staring directly at me. I looked the dog in his eyes and said, " The Blood of Jesus," Right then, I heard a man call out to the dog, and he turned right back around and went back inside his yard. Lord have mercy, I was tripping! I looked again, and the dog (which was bigger than me) no longer looked like a wolf but a huge German shepherd. At that moment, I knew it was an attack from the enemy.

There were many situations where I knew the enemy was working. One time I was preparing to go to an event that was an hour-long drive, and as I was driving, I felt my car stuttering on the freeway a few times. I thought to myself, oh man, Lord, please let me make it to my destination safe and sound. I'd had a couple of cars broken down in the past. One of those times, my cousin, her one-month-old baby, and I were on a freeway, and my transmission blew out. While waiting for someone to come to our rescue, someone shot a flare gun into the air and caused a wildfire! Thanks be to God, we got out of there before it got worse. However, we did end up staying overnight at my grandmother's Pastor and family's home. As you can imagine, this was something I did not want to experience again! As my car stalled on the freeway, I thought it would be good to have a newer car, so I wouldn't have to worry about it breaking down, especially while I had my kids. One week, my mother came for a visit. We went out to eat that morning, and as we pulled up to my house, she asked out of the blue, "How long have you had your car?" I told her about nine years. She said, "Well, you have been such a good girl; I think it's about time for you to have another one. She said, "Pray about it and see what God says." When my mother said I had been "such a good girl", she meant I had been faithful to God, the best wife I knew how to be, and a good mother to our children.

The next day, while I was sitting down at my dining room table, I spent time with God in prayer, and right before I ended, I asked God, "Lord, you know that I have been having problems with my car, and it is going to take thousands of dollars to get it fixed. We do not have the finances to put down as a down payment; therefore, I would like to know if I could have permission to get another car?" I was hoping to use my car as a down payment and have a black car. I continued to pray, and I asked that my car note payments be lower than what I had been paying before. Just as I was finishing up my prayer, my brother or sister, a text message came through. I checked the message. It said, "I love you." This message came from a friend who didn't know what was happening at the time. I said, "Oh My God! Are you saying it's okay to get another car?"

I called my mother and explained what had happened. She said that it was confirmation; the Lord was saying, "Yes." We made arrangements the next day, along with her long-time friend, to start my search for another vehicle. My car was drivable, but it would slow down from time to time, and as we drove to the dealership, I had another issue and had to drive really slowly.

Needless to say, it was time for another car. When we got to the dealership, I called my husband. Our conversation went exactly as I expected. Not good at all. He wasn't happy at all. I asked him if he had any objections to me just looking around, and he said no, *grudgingly*. Lol. I looked at a car that I thought would be the cheapest car on sale. But it was different from what I had seen online. The car looked so small; my youngest son could fit in there alone. Lol. So, of course, I had to look at a bigger car. We saw another vehicle that was the right size for the kids and I. I test drove it around the area and then behind the dealership.

We went to sit down at one of the desks, and a professional young lady sat down on the other side and started tapping on the computer. While we were waiting for her technician to come back with how much they would give me for the car, she began to tell me they would give me the manufacturer's price of the new car instead of the sticker price. She also said that they would give me two thousand dollars for the rebate, another twelve hundred dollars based on the area I lived in, along with four-thousand dollars for my old car. That's not all; I would get an employee discount because of my job, an additional five hundred dollars off the liability insurance, and on top of that, my payments were going to be one hundred dollars less than what I had previously paid! As the young lady was laying out all of the discounts, my mother looked as if she was about to fall out of the chair she was sitting in! Her friend had a look of surprise on his face as well! I sat there thinking to myself, "Wow, God, you really do love me that much!!!" It was so unbelievable what was happening; there was no way I could say no to that deal. I accepted the deal, and as they were preparing to get my vehicle ready for me, I waited in the little waiting area and remembered thinking, "Oh my God! What am I going to say to my husband? He is not going to be happy with me?" Just as I was thinking this, I got a text message at that moment from the same person who texted me the day before saying, "When a man's ways please the Lord, He makes even his enemies to be at peace with him." **Proverbs 16:7, KJV** My brother or sister, I was just SOOO astonished, I was so in awe of God! There was no doubt in my mind that God was guiding and comforting me all at the same time!

God made it to where I could not deny what they were offering me. There was no way I could say no. I didn't wake up one day and say, " Oh, I'm going to go buy a new car, " knowing our current situation. This wasn't even on my list of priorities. As far as I was concerned, this was the favor of God! On this, I give God all the Glory!

CHAPTER FOURTEEN

My Heavenly Language

"AND when the day of Pentecost was fully come, they were all with one accord in one place. And suddenly there came a sound from heaven as of a rushing mighty wind, and it filled all the house where they were sitting. And there appeared unto them cloven tongues like as of fire, and it sat upon each of them. And they were all filled with the Holy Ghost, and began to speak with other tongues, as the Spirit gave them utterance.

ACTS 2:1-4, KJV

About five or six years ago, I was curious about speaking in tongues, but I didn't understand what speaking in tongues entailed. I heard other people speaking in their heavenly language, but I never really thought about it coming up. I was brought up in a Baptist church, and there were certain beliefs about speaking in an unknown tongue. This was something that we did not practice, so there was no need to understand at the time. However, have you ever wondered if there is more to just going to Church Sunday after Sunday? Have you ever felt like something is missing, like there should be more power, hunger, and thirst for God? I know I can't be the only one who ever felt this way. Something on the inside was telling me I was missing the mark.

I remember a discussion in Bible study at my Church. We were in the book of Acts; something about the book of Acts attracts my spirit. It's like an awakening takes place every time I read anything in the book of Acts; it feels like something inside me is activated. I became curious as to why no one believed in the power of speaking in their heavenly language *through the Holy Spirit.* I could not understand why we read something in Scripture about Jesus, saying that it is a gift to us, but we didn't practice it? I started asking God about this. I wanted to know what speaking in tongues was about and the purpose of us having this *heavenly* language? I wanted to know how it would benefit us by speaking in other unknown tongues. I heard from others that speaking in tongues was gibberish and of no value to them. Some would not give heed to opening their mouths and making crazy sounds that didn't make any sense to them or anyone else. They talked about how some think that it's of the devil, which in some cases would be *if you are not in the right Spirit.* The enemy will always try to imitate what God has called good and pervert it, just like he has perverted everything else that God has created. Still, I couldn't move the thought from my mind.

Two things in the Bible stood out to me. One was, "But this is that which was spoken by the prophet Joel; and it shall come to pass in the last days, saith God, that I will pour out of my Spirit upon all flesh: and your sons and your daughters shall prophesy (preach), and your young men shall see visions, and your old men shall dream dreams: And on my servants and on my handmaidens I will pour out in those days of My Spirit; and they shall prophesy:" **Acts 2:16-18, KJV** At first, when I read this scripture, I was in a place of confusion because I thought that we did have His Spirit. I didn't realize that He was talking about the Baptism of the Holy Ghost. He sure wasn't talking about the day of Pentecost because what the disciples had experienced was just the beginning. Jesus had to ascend to heaven for them to receive the Holy Ghost with the evidence of speaking in tongues. Then, the scripture said, "...upon all flesh in the last days; His Spirit will be poured out" God is talking about every person of all ages, male or female, children included. So, that means God is talking about us today, right now, so I continued to inquire about this. It took some time because I needed someone to teach me and I had to study on my own as well.

The Lord opened up the door for me to learn more about the Baptism of the Holy Ghost. According to Scripture, He equips believers to witness and minister. The Holy Spirit gives the believer supernatural power and ability **(Luke 10:19, KJV),** enabling them to fulfill God's calling effectively. He is the Power that enables us in our mission to represent Jesus. I learned that even Jesus was full of the Holy Ghost **(Luke 4:1, KJV)** as he was led in the wilderness. I don't think I realized this until it was brought to my attention; you see, it's the little details that make a difference when studying the Word. I thought to myself, Ohhhh!! I get it; now it makes even more sense how Jesus was able to be bold in the things that He was able to do. The second part that stuck out concerning the day of Pentecost was how the disciples were all filled with the Holy Ghost and how God said that we have the gift already on the inside of us, and if we wanted it, all we had to do was receive it. For most of us, when we come to accept Jesus Christ as our personal Savior, we have the baptism with the Spirit that occurs once at salvation, the filling of the Holy Spirit occurs after the believer is saved. The baptism of the Holy Spirit occurs only once, while the *filling* of the Spirit occurs many times. The Baptism of the Holy Spirit sets the stage for a filling of the Spirit, which the believer directly experiences.

What the Holy Spirit does for you is helps you in every aspect of your life. Before Jesus left and ascended into Heaven, He told the disciples that He would send a Helper, and a Comforter, to help them. What I've learned about the Holy Spirit is that we have to give Him permission to breakthrough in our lives! When we begin to speak in unknown languages, we will have the boldness to share the gospel like never before! When you give the Holy Spirit permission to manifest in your life, the gift that was always there in your life will now begin to thrust forward. You will become more confident like Peter did when He preached the gospel to thousands of people. You get more clarity---the gift of discerning spirits. You may have the gift of administration and begin to have a revelation of these gifts. Now, the Word of God comes alive to you because you are now reading it through the lenses of the Holy Spirit.

And most importantly, the Holy Spirit helps you grow fruit--lookup **(Galatians 5:22-23, KJV).** We learn how God speaks to us, renews our mind to pray perfect prayers at all times, and build us up on our most Holy faith **(Jude 1:20, KJV),** which is an advantage. He leads us to do the things God has called us to do, which will always involve the miraculous because we are powerless to do anything. We get filled with the Holy Spirit to dominate the earth and take over the areas that we've been called to. When you get filled with the Holy Spirit, it takes you to a whole different level!

As I sit and think back, I recall going to a women's conference called "*When the Vow Breaks.*" There was an Evangelist there preaching her soul out, giving her testimony of how the Lord brought her out of some severe circumstances and how she endured those hard and challenging times. As we were standing and praising the Lord, I had fixed my hair in my natural short curly state with a flower clipped on the left side of my hair. I was sitting way in the back of the room when she pointed me out. She said to me, "God wants to take you higher in Him." She said, "The enemy is trying to put your mind into a state of depression that goes back seven years, but God wants you to come up higher in Him." The Evangelist was right on point with the timing, but I didn't quite connect the dots. I took what she said to the Lord and asked what exactly did He mean? *Well, about three years later, I finally figured it out.* One morning, I'd just gotten off from work from an incredibly stressful night shift. I got home around eight a.m. and took a hot bath. I used this time to unwind and play some gospel music on Pandora. I began to spend some time with God and started telling Him that I was ready to be baptized in the Holy Ghost with the evidence of speaking in tongues. Then, the Lord brought it to my remembrance, what He had spoken three years ago.

I took a deep breath, and finally, I realized what God wanted me to do. I was ready, and I wanted Him to bring me up higher! As I prayed and praised Him, the songs playing were so in sync with what I was praying. *Fill Me Up God*, songs by Casey J. played, but when *Hallelujah* by Tamela Mann, started to play, the Lord baptized me in the Holy Ghost, and my heavenly language broke through!!! I tell you, my brother or sister, it was such an incredible experience, I almost couldn't believe it, but it was actually happening right in the middle of the lukewarm water that I was in! I was hearing it for the first time, and I was speaking in tongues through the Holy Spirit with no understanding as to what I was saying, but it didn't matter---I believed that I had received the baptism of the Holy Ghost by the evidence of tongues! I believe I was thanking God in my new language, and I just continued to praise God! I felt as if I was floating. By the time I looked up at the clock, it was a quarter to eleven! I was wrinkled when I got out of the tub, but I didn't care; I felt light as a feather, but my feet were wobbling like a baby taking their first steps. I took a nap, and when I woke up, I felt so full! I can only explain it as the feeling you get after eating an entire meal, with seconds! It was a satisfying fullness in my belly like I'd had enough to carry me until the next day —it was just so amazing!

I began to pray every day in the Spirit, meaning in my new language. Although it sounded like I was babbling, I noticed a difference in how I was speaking. The more I spoke, the more apparent the difference in the sounds and syllables were until the "words" came in full fledge. At that time, I had yet to know what God was going to do, but I sure wanted to be ready for whatever He purposed for me to do! In the Name of Jesus, I will do whatever He says. I am looking forward to the Power of God manifesting Himself through me. Glory to God! I now understand why those who are newly saved are not conscious of the Holy Spirit inside them. Still, they have a connection with their soul, and they know enough to say, "I'm born again according to the Word of God. If I believe in my heart that God raised Jesus from the dead and confess with my mouth that Jesus is Lord, I will be saved." Many stop there because that may be the only thing they are conscious of. So, they never move on to anything else in the realm of the Spirit. Please understand my brother or sister; I'm not coming down on those who aren't baptized in the Holy Spirit with the evidence of speaking in tongues. I, too, came into this knowledge later in life. It wasn't until I read that Jesus said I could have the Holy Ghost, I studied the power manifested in scripture (I've read it many times), and the Word of God illuminated my mind that I had this understanding. Something sparked in my spirit, and I agreed with His word. I wanted what God had for me; my hunger for His word increased.

It's hard to explain this to anyone who may not be interested in understanding this. Still, the Bible speaks a lot about praying in the Holy Ghost with the evidence of other tongues as the Spirit gives utterance. The Holy Spirit, also called the Holy Ghost, is not a feeling or an it, but a person. For those seeking to be baptized in the Holy Ghost with the evidence of speaking in tongues or are interested in this, may I encourage you to seek the Lord to be filled with the gift of the Holy Spirit and gain more understanding? I believe this will bless you, and it will benefit you. This is a gift Jesus gives to all those who **believe in Him**. Praying in the Spirit has helped me tremendously when I just don't know what to pray for, how to pray for something or someone, or run out of things to pray, as your spirit prays, it is praying a perfect prayer. **Please refer to (Romans 8:26-27, KJV)** There are times I may pray for things I need rather than what the Lord knows I need. But in the Spirit, God knows everything, so my spirit and God's Spirit are working together in getting a prayer through. Now, I am asking God for the interpretation of what I am praying for.

In the midst of all I was facing, the Lord filled me with His Holy Spirit. I tell you; this was the best feeling I've ever had in my life as well as the best gift God could ever give to His children besides His son Jesus Christ. There is no better experience in the world than being able to be in tune with my Heavenly Father. This was the missing link for me!

CHAPTER FIFTEEN

The Missing Link!

It was now time for our women's retreat again. My God, what an incredible time I had; it was such an eye-opener for me. I wish everyone reading these testimonies could understand why I was so excited! If you could understand what it cost me to stand while enduring these tests, that could have very well taken me out had I not held on to my Father! The enemy tried everything he could to destroy my life, marriage, kids, and husband, so the women's retreat was timely and had always been a safe place for me. Honestly, with all I was going through, I could have found my way to a club, drinking, committing adultery, anything to keep my mind occupied from the issues I was having at home, Church, and work! It was becoming increasingly stressful just dealing with everyday life. I had no choice but to live through it and stand; while I was standing, I sought God for everything. He is the one who has all the answers, and as I sought God, I would receive them. He may not have answered me when I asked Him, but His answer was always right on time! "But they that wait upon the LORD, the Lord shall renew their strength; they shall mount up with wings as eagles; they shall run, and not be weary, and they shall walk, and not faint." **Isaiah 40:31, KJV**

Speaking of answered prayers, God gave me confirmation after confirmation. Another word was given to me by another Evangelist at the women's retreat I attended. She called me out and said, "Woman of God, it's time to start walking in your authority. God is going to use you; you are going to do some things that will be so magnificent and mighty in God." She said, "God is going to have you doing things that will shock your family, walk into your authority!" Then, she began to pray for me. As she laid hands on me, I fell back, but thankfully there were women at the altar who caught me. I laid out on the floor and began praising God in my Heavenly Language! I thought what I was feeling a month prior when I received my Heavenly Language the first time was something. My God!! I have never felt so drunk in the Spirit!

Not only that, but while I was still on the floor, it was apparent that the Evangelist was on the floor with me, because I heard her speak into my left ear. She said to me again, "Walk into your authority; even your family will know God is using you.." I remember her saying, " Walk into the newness, everything will be new; it's time to walk into the new. Step into the new. Your family will see how God is using you." I thought it was so weird that I could still hear what she was saying to me while lying there still in the Spirit. I heard what the Lord was speaking through her so *clearly*. When I tried to get up off the floor, someone had to help me because the power of God was so strong; I felt so drunk and practically slid off the chair being so deep in the Spirit. I mean, I could not stop; it was rolling off my tongue so heavy. This was a high I never wanted to come down from! It was God having a serious one on one with me. There is no way I could miss this moment or get out of it! I ***needed*** to stay in this ***meeting*** with my Lord!

I missed so much of what happened in that service! Lol, The enemy was getting beat up left and right! He couldn't stand being in that room with the mothers praying and being used by God to help set people free! I tell you, no demon in hell is a match for the power of God! Later in the service, some of us were asked to testify about our experience that night. Normally, I would not have gotten up to speak unless I was asked to. But this night, I volunteered to get up and give my testimony. I don't recall everything I said word for word, but I do remember telling the saints that I had been seeking the Holy Ghost with the evidence of speaking in tongues. I told them when I was filled with His Spirit; I realized that this had been the missing link! Now, I see why the enemy doesn't want God's people to get their Heavenly Language. It's the tool we need to go forth in the ministry when being used by God!

The next day was Sunday morning; some sisters in Christ and I ate breakfast, and we headed to their Church *(which is like my second home church)* to fellowship. Oh, my goodness! The presence of God was there in that building; the whole Church was giving God all the Glory! As I was praising the Lord, the woman of God, the same Evangelist that spoke to me the night before, jumped directly in front of me and said, "God is going to fix it for you." Lord have mercy, that caused me to run around the Church then! Lol. You know when God is speaking to you! The person speaking to may not know why they are saying what they are saying, they simply allow God to use them to tell you what He wants you to know. However, I knew exactly what she was referring to. Now, mind you, I had never spoken with any of these women of God. I had never had a one-on-one conversation with these people, let alone seen them before, as they all lived out of state. When service was over, we greeted each other, and she said to me again, "Hey, woman of God! God is going to fix a couple of things for you." She told me, "Just begin to thank Him for fixing it for you. Even when it looks like it's worse because it's not what it seems, just keep giving Him thanks."

After that blessed weekend, I had a chance to reflect on what had transpired; it reminded me of when I spoke with one of my spiritual mentors, who was very straightforward; she did not pull any punches with me concerning the things of God. At times, she would give me a word from the Lord concerning the future. I didn't quite understand why she shared certain things because I didn't know what the Lord was leading me into during this time, but here I was! I now understood why God did what He did the following weekend. So, the Spirit of God led my mentor to tell me to remain humble and not think that I am better than anyone else. She said to always say that it is God and not me. I am just His vessel being used for His Glory. She said I am to remain blameless, be the same sweet person I've always been, and continue to give people hugs and bless them. She emphasized not to think that you are above anyone because God can sit you down just as quickly. STAY HUMBLE, STAY HUMBLE!!!! She would tell me adamantly, "Just go where God sends you. God will equip you for where He is taking you." So, I said to God, "Wherever You are taking me, just equip me to do Your work and Your Will."

"Verily, verily, I say unto you, He that believeth on Me, the works that I do shall he do also; and greater works than these shall he do; because I go unto My Father." **(John 14:12, KJV)**

This was another revelation of why the enemy had been trying to destroy me and everything around me. He did not want me to know who I am in Christ Jesus, and he wanted to keep me so distracted that I would not find out the plan of God for my life. Now, I understood why the lady at Church told me not to give up, and I sensed that she could see in the Spirit. I knew God was speaking to me, and I fully understand why God doesn't want to give us His plans all at once. It would have consumed me. Each time I got a revelation from God, it was like He was taking me to the next chapter, the next journey, and the next level. Everything I was going through was like a test that I had to pass. If I did not pass, I would have to stay there until I passed the test before moving on to the next thing, which is why it would not take *me* long to follow instructions! One thing that I had to learn throughout this process was to be obedient. Obedience made the process so much easier to go through!

I spoke with a Pastor one afternoon regarding something I needed. Somehow our conversation turned unexpectedly and he gave me some advice. He told me that God is preparing me for ministry, so I would have to tell my husband when the time came. I'm thinking to myself, how and when will I be able to tell him something like that?! I said to myself, God, **you** will have to ***open up that door*** when that time comes.

CHAPTER SIXTEEN

A Strategic Decision

As you can see, my brother or sister, after years of going through challenges in my household, I would sit and wonder why I felt like I had been in this predicament before. I started thinking about my life from the beginning. I thought about my younger years and the things I've endured. It almost felt like I was in the same circumstance, but the only difference was it wasn't the same person, and I was now an adult. You would have thought my husband and I had purposely done something to cause our lives to be in such turmoil. Some people may think it's normal and that everyone has issues in their families and lives. People may want to believe, "things happen," and may say, "it is what it is," but when it comes to my marriage and family, the devil is a liar, and he *cannot* tell the truth **(John 8:44, KJV).** Anyone else's thoughts would have been irrelevant; there was nothing "normal" about what we were going through. The enemy had done his best to keep us distracted, so we wouldn't know that God had a purpose for us as individuals, as a couple, and as a family. However, the time had now come for me to say enough is enough!!! Things were so out of control in our lives that getting up as a family and attending church had become difficult. At this point, our lives were on total display (and not in a positive way) for everyone in our church and family to see; it was nothing but the power of the Holy Spirit that kept me from totally breaking down and falling apart! One afternoon, while at home, I broke down and prayed so hard! I asked God to give me an outlet because our issues were noticeable, and they were becoming unbearable. God had to come to my rescue because what I thought of doing would have made things a little more complicated for me and a bit easier for the enemy to gain more territory into our lives! I wanted to quietly walk away and let the marriage go, but God would not open the door to remove myself from our marriage and home how I desired. My decision to leave really made sense to me at the time, but if I had not listened to God's directions to ***remain in our home***, it probably would have taken longer for us to come to a resolution. I thought to myself, well, God, you want me to stay; it's time for me to go on another three-day fast to find out the next move to make.

One of the main reasons I needed to fast was because, during the process of developing my relationship with God, I felt boxed in. I loved witnessing the miracles and wonders I saw Him do, seeing the prayers He was answering, and experiencing the joy and peace I would feel just by being in His presence. I loved where I was with God, and honestly, I desired to share all these things with my husband, but we just weren't seeing eye to eye. When your heart has been hardened like cement, how can it be broken up? It would take God's power and authority to give us the breakthrough we needed in our marriage. It was also going to require hard work, surrender, and a lot of forgiveness. When cement is wet, you have to smoothen it out. When it dries up, it dries up with whatever has been mixed with it. In our case, it was a lot of clutter and confusion, which would take ***salt*** to break it up with a healthy dose of ***repentance***. I knew that the testimony would be great once the bondages were broken! Jesus is the *SALT*!!! But who was going to be the **one to surrender?**

I was now on day one of my three-day fast. I needed God to tell me what steps to take because things were beyond out of control. It looked like the enemy had gained so much territory, and honestly, it seemed almost impossible to put the pieces back together. I could no longer deal with what was taking place, which is why I continued to seek God. Truthfully speaking, my life depended on it.

"For with God nothing shall be impossible" **Luke 1:37, KJV**

Upon ending the three-day fast, I heard in my spirit, "You can remove yourself now." I'm looking around like, did I hear you, right Lord? What do you mean? At first, I thought He was telling me to move out and get another apartment, but as I pondered on this statement, I felt God was telling me to take my hands out of things (remove myself), He will deal with my circumstances. Had I done what I thought the Lord was saying and not meditated on it, I would have made the wrong choice. I know this to be true because, in the midst of that thought, the Lord said, "NO! If you leave, the enemy will gain more territory in your home." So, I could not do that. As a last result, I would at least attend another church, *but that wasn't the answer, either.*

Some time ago, I was standing in the middle of my living room, and I felt this uneasiness in my spirit. I got down on my knees; I said to God, "I don't know what is getting ready to happen, but whatever it is that I need to be prepared for, please help me deal with it. Protect me and my children, keep us safe." I knew something would happen; I just didn't know who, what, how, or when. I just *knew* I needed to be *ready* for it. "But God hath chosen the foolish things of the world to confound the wise, and God hath chosen the weak things of the world to confound the things which are mighty;" **(1 Corinthians 1:27, KJV)**

Now, here is another moment of transparency that I must share for God to be glorified in my testimony. The thought came to me to file for a divorce. The topic was brought up on many occasions, not because we wanted to part ways; we just couldn't seem to come together, but I believe God wanted to do something through that situation. One night, as I was lying down in my bed, I went back and forth with God about the decisions I had to make. I said, "Lord, I don't understand why you just won't fix our marriage while we're still married and living together in the home? I don't want to add anything else to what's already being said about us publicly. Can't we go through this privately?" You see, I believe God gave us chance after chance to get it right on our own. It had already been a long journey; it was only a matter of time before we came down this road. Today I understand that *God's Plan is not based on our feelings, but* I felt like this was my only choice during that time. After all, a family divided against itself cannot stand."...Every kingdom divided against itself is brought to desolation, and every city or house divided against itself shall not stand:" **(Matthew 12:25, KJV).** Needless to say, *I fell asleep with a lot on my mind.*

What I am about to share with you may sound strange but the next morning, when I opened my eyes, I felt a sense of peace simply because I was prepared for whatever way things went. If we went through the entire dissolution process or reconciled, I would be okay. Not only did I have peace about my future, but I woke up with answers to all of the questions I had the night before. I knew the direction to take and who to call, but honestly, I was scared. My brother or sister, this decision was not made without prayer and serious consideration for the church and our children. Yes, I could have left things the way they were and suffered through it, but I believe things would have been much worse if I had stayed. We could no longer remain in this place of despair. Too much was at stake, it was now or never, and something had to give. So, I filed for divorce. Yes, I know God hates divorce; I hate it too! However, for **us** to come to a place of healing, things had to get worse before they could get better, but at this point, felt like things couldn't get any worse than they already were. *I felt at peace with my decision*, and that God knew what would come of all this. I truly felt my hands were tied.

After I filed...boy oh boy! The enemy thought it was a wrap, and I'm sure he was happy it happened. To be honest with you, even though I was not happy about going through the process of getting a divorce, I felt relieved. I felt like I was able to breathe for the first time in a very long time. Our marriage had been in turmoil for so long; I was just glad something was being done. I am just being honest. Now don't get me wrong, this was not easy by a long shot; I truly believe God sent me some extra Angels to get me through this rough patch.

CHAPTER SEVENTEEN

I Never Took My Ring Off

You never want to be someone people are whispering about, and I know that many who know me personally will read my story. I'm sure there were a lot of questions, like why couldn't they stay together? I am sure statements were made like, "They **were** such a cute couple. Some may have said, but this cute couple didn't show any fruit of being a cute couple. They were supposed to believe in God. But many had no idea how viciously the enemy was fighting us, and he wasn't fighting fair! Of course, we had our part to play. I prayed, I fast, but let's be honest, when you're married to a pastor, it takes an army of prayer warriors to cover not only him but his entire house. As a body of believers, it is imperative to stand in the gap, not just for your Pastor but for all who are in trouble. Now, I'm not saying that no one prayed or stood in the gap for us outside those who came to me directly. What I do know is that the warfare spilled into church. Believe it or not, I felt like God had given me the grace to withstand the fires we would embark on. I felt God's strength every step of the way, and I knew God had my back the entire time.

After I made the decision, were there some reservations? Yes, of course. I didn't have any more tears left to shed. That's how much strength God had given me. One day, as we were going through this process, I wondered if I should take my ring off? I know I filed for a divorce, but I didn't know what to do! I figured it was better that I kept it on, considering that this could put me in an even more vulnerable position; after all, there were occasions when a few people tried to approach me even with my ring on. I had to be mindful to protect myself from getting into a compromising situation. I didn't have time for things to become more complicated, but that's not it; I also believed in my heart that things were not over.

I remembered all the things God told me. He said He would deal with my husband and reveal things in His own time and for me to keep standing. He told me that all of our lives were going to ***change like never before***. One day, in particular, an elderly mother was praying around me; she said that she heard the word 'healing' for me twice. At that moment, the Lord reminded me that I would no longer be cooped up in my room. It was time to come out and praise the Lord, and no one would be able to stop me! He also reminded me of what fell in my spirit another time. He said we would both go in different directions, but eventually, He would bring us back together. I believe that word was multifaceted and that it also meant spiritually. He reminded me that a prayer of complete deliverance had been prayed over my husband and that I was to wait and see the manifestation of those prayers that had gone forth. The Lord reminded me on many occasions that healing would take place.

He was still my husband, and I still had to stand in the gap on his behalf. Even though we didn't act like we were married, in the eyes of God, we made a covenant before Him. We made a pledge before Him to have and to hold from this day forward, for better or for worse, for richer, for poorer, in sickness and in health, to love and to cherish, till death do us part according to

God's Holy ordinance. *Therefore, I never took off my ring.* Now, this may seem strange, but I felt I loved my husband even more during this time. It was as if God had given me another set of eyes to see him differently. This was a hard battle to fight, especially when I felt like I was the only one fighting it. When the enemy has you blinded, you can't see anything, and you only think you know what you need to know; I don't believe my husband knew all the tricks the enemy had up his sleeves, but I saw things ***clearly***. It took years for things to unfold. As I kept my mind on Jesus, more was being exposed. It was really difficult going through and with the church. I do feel that some wanted to ask questions but did not want to seem as if they were prying.

I also believe some had the "oh well, marriages don't last long nowadays" mentality and figured, what's one more *failed marriage?* In some cases, people feel you should just pretend you're okay and just play your part. On the other hand, some don't care to see a marriage survive. In every situation, there are two sides to the story. You cannot fully understand until you put both pieces of the story together. Then, one can see how the enemy got in, when, and who he got in through. Truth be told, even if others knew the details of what transpired, nobody but God could fix this situation. Ultimately, God knows the truth, and only He knows what the outcome will be. We just have to go through it and come out as pure as gold!

"But He knoweth the way that I take: when He hath tried me, I shall come forth as gold. **(Job 23:10, KJV)** in some translations, it says, 'I shall come out as pure as gold.'

Here is a ***FLASHBACK MOMENT***

In the realm of the spirit, a Pastor saw the enemy conspiring against our family during a Pastor's anniversary service for my husband. The enemy wanted to exclude me out of the equation, but this was one of those days that I was not having it. Satan (...because we don't wrestle with flesh and blood according to Ephesians 6:12) was throwing all kinds of fiery darts from every angle and his plan almost succeeded. I actually left before the service even started because of the treatment I received. I was being talked down to as if I didn't belong, but immediately after this transpired, I was able to connect the dots and find out what was really happening behind the scenes, and I tell you, I was left flabbergasted. To be honest, that was a trick from the enemy to make me believe that I was only supposed to make an "appearance" to make my husband look good, but I had no intention of being the "First Lady" everybody wanted me to portray. What would be the point of standing in a role if I could not be my true self? Of course, I would conduct myself the way I had always done my whole life, in that same church I called "My Safe Haven," but this was one of those days I was simply tired of all the foolishness.

It took a couple of people to call me on my drive home and pray me through. As I was being prayed over, I heard the Lord say to me, "Go back." So, I drove all the way home, only to turn around and go back to the church! You talk about the Holy Spirit arresting you! Whew! Now I was still upset, but I knew the Lord was right in saying go back. At that moment, I could think clearly and I realized that this was a part of the enemy's agenda to make it seem as if I had no desire to support my husband. If he could do that, then, of course some would have their confirmation that I wasn't in support of him. So, I had to go back, no matter how ugly it looked. I had to sit next to my husband, feeling hotter than fish grease, and as uncomfortable as I was, I was being obedient to God, but things continued to get worse. All in all, I did what I had been asked to do and was on my ***best behavior***. It cost me a lot to sit there in the midst of that madness and humiliation.

Many don't understand the bondage they try to inflict on the ones they call the 'First Lady.' Many believe her only purpose is to conduct herself in a fashionable manner and make her husband, the Pastor look good. You are to be a good girl and pretend that everything is alright. Now, I understand that you must walk in maturity and not cause a scene; that is not an issue. What was hurtful is, I felt that there weren't many who genuinely cared about the hurt I was feeling. In fact, we weren't genuine about anything, not even at that moment, with all that drama, the service was no longer about God! I remember saying to myself, what happened to my Safe Haven? I no longer felt safe. I could no longer feel God's presence there, and it was just too much to bear.

After service, the tension was so thick that another Pastor's wife came over to encourage me. I was so grateful for her insight because she didn't know me. As we were in one corner, she continued to encourage me but I could see someone talking to another person who was not a member of our church. The art of reading lips can come in very handy when you need to know something. I wasn't looking for it, but the disdain was so evident; how could I have missed it? It was on display for everyone to see as well.

A Thought To Consider…

Now, mind you, we are talking about a body of believers, not non-believers still in the world. There was so much division and confusion in the church, and no one knew what the enemy was trying to distract us from, but glory be to God; there is always a solution to our problems!

While God was dealing with my husband and me separately, I believe God was also dealing with **His** Church. Satan, the devil, the thief that kills, steals, and destroys who does not tell the truth, wanted to destroy our church. Satan went through many different avenues to tear down what God had built for so many years. We were up and down for so long; it was like we were riding on a rollercoaster, but I knew in my heart that God had something much greater for our church, if only we could just be on one accord! If only we could see in the spirit what God wanted to do with this body of Christ!

CHAPTER EIGHTEEN

The Breakthrough Has Finally Arrived

I could see the heart of God when a vow is broken between a husband and wife. God and Jesus are one, Jesus and the Church are one. God the Father, the Son, and the Holy Ghost are one. I mentioned this because I have learned a tremendous number of lessons over the years. From the time I said, "I do," in my marriage vows, to the time I said, "Yes," to God, that I will do whatever He planned for me to do for His Kingdom; to fight with the enemy in order to keep my sanity, peace, and my joy. In all of this, I truly learned to become one with God. When I said, "I do," to my husband, I knew we would have ups and downs as all marriages have, so that was to be expected. I didn't expect the route that it took to become one with each other. Being married shows you a side of your personality that you did not know you had. It brings out your good side, your nice side, your mean side, your ugly side, your secret side, your I don't care side, your I'm not in love with you side, your conditional love side, your you do it yourself side and even your leave me alone side. LOL

This is why God gave us His holy scriptures so we would know how to act towards one another. I find that we go back and forth between our feelings and how we want things to be versus how and what the scriptures instruct us to do when it comes to being married. We, sometimes, pick and choose what we want out of the Bible to defend the way we act towards one another. When one spouse is acting "unspiritual," the other spouse gets in their feelings, and instead of doing what the word of God says, they treat them the same way they are being treated.

Most of us want love with all the trimmings; I wish that would have been the case in our situation. I would have been in a world of trouble if I wasn't prepared for all of the chaos, drama, blended family issues, roommate status, financial dilemmas, and the negative outside influences! Now, was I expecting my marriage to look like this? NO. Nor was I preparing to go through these exact issues. What I am saying is, before we get into marriage, I think it is critical that we make a decision to strive to love ***God's way,*** instead of picking and choosing how we're going to love our spouse. Remember, you have two different personalities joining into one sacred covenant marriage union. You have to understand that it is going to take the power of God to make the marriage union work. But it requires that both spouses put in a lot of hard work. It's a choice. It is not easy, ***but it is possible.***

I sometimes use this analogy---if you have five hundred puzzle pieces and each spouse has two hundred and fifty pieces, they both have a job to put the puzzle together. It is up to them to bring the puzzle to life and display the picture on top of the box. So, they start around the edges. Those are easy; you can pull all the edges out and put those together without much of a problem. Let's use the edges as an analogy for when you first meet your spouse, and you're getting to know one another for the first time. In the beginning, you only want them to know the good side of you. Next, you try to make things a little easier by separating the pieces, maybe by color code or a tree you put that together. If there is a house, you put those pieces together, or perhaps a car, you try to put those pieces together because those pieces are most evident. However, there are many pieces, and they are pretty small, so it takes a while to find the matching pieces. Now, everyone knows that two heads are better than one. So, if you try to put the puzzle together alone, it's going to take you a while to finish, and maybe some of you will not even finish; you just may give up and come back to it another time. Others may give up altogether and not come back at all. There are some who don't give up; they go all in until the whole puzzle is put together, but ultimately, it's up to both teammates (spouses) to help finish until the end.

"...the race is not to the swift, nor the strong, but time and chance happeneth to them all." **Ecclesiastes 9:11, KJV**

"But he that shall endure unto the end, the same shall be saved." **Matthew 24:13, KJV**

Everything that has transpired over the years looked impossible. But let me tell you, ***My Heavenly Father*** came through!!! He saved my marriage just like He promised He would! God made the impossible possible! He made a way out of no way, just like He opened the Red Sea for the Israelites! He even opened up the hearts of our family! I'm amazed at what God has done for us! I wanted our marriage restoration to be quiet, easy, smooth, and ***private***. Here's the thing, we can be ashamed of many things that took place in our lives, but God chose what was foolish to the world to shame the wise, and He took my pain and turned it into Purpose! These things did not make sense to me at first, but as the process continued, God began to give me an understanding of why things had to go the way they did. My brother or sister, I believe it was necessary to go through this process in order for us to arrive at ***God's*** expected end.

The first point I want to share is this wasn't just about how God restored our marriage. This was about what it takes to ***stay*** in the fight with God's help without giving up so easily, because I almost did on several occasions, only because I didn't fully know who I was in Christ or who and why I was fighting?!

The second point I want to make is that it took a divine process of being trained by God to truly know who I am in Him and not focus on my marriage itself (the tree). I needed to see what the enemy was trying to stop and destroy, which was the bigger picture (the forest).

My third point is that if I had given up, I would have to start the process all over again; even though we were going through the trial of dissolution, it was all based on trusting God with ***His Strategic Plan*** to come to ***His expected end.*** This required and brought about complete trust in God. I am not saying that you will get the same results if you do all these. I cannot speak for anyone else's decisions about saving their marriage; only what I know had taken place for me. I believe that even if I weren't married, the enemy would have still found a way to distract me. There would have been all kinds of situations that would have taken place. I could have been sleeping around with someone who wasn't my husband, being physically abused, or still going to clubs, drinking, and while attending church. Instead, I ended up with this **test**imony, but how else would I know that God can do the impossible? I went into my marriage determined to give my best in everything. I didn't know how I would do that, but I knew I would keep God in the middle. I didn't know that God had other plans for me, my husband, and our children as well.

We are now almost fourteen years in! I'm not even sure if I would have agreed to go through the trials, we have faced had I known we would have to face them. I am just being honest! Lol, I can see why people want to be blessed and used by God but don't want to go through the process of being blessed and used. But seriously, it's a guarantee that this walk and your marriage ***will cost you something***, but you don't know what or how much??? Be ready to be tested on all counts: your character, integrity, sanity, friendships, family, emotions, heart, tongue, mind, peace, and your...? *You fill in the blank!*

May I stress the fact that Satan ***HATES*** marriages and will do everything possible to break up what God has put together? One of the things I was reminded of is when the time comes that I will come face to face with God, I will have to give an account of how I treated my husband. He is still a child of God. He is a man of God. I also learned that we must be careful how we treat other people. You never know how the Lord can and will use a person. You speak against them; you speak against God. We need to learn to pray for those who are experiencing hard times. You could very well be the one that Satan is using to tear down something or someone you should be praying for, or you could be the very one that God uses to help restore and make right through your righteous and true prayers. The choice is yours. What happens is, you create an open door for the enemy to enter into your spirit when you choose the former.

We must come to repentance and salvation. It is critical that we do this. It is time for people to be delivered from many different bondages and learn to keep their deliverance. God wants to break those spirits of anger, bitterness, molestation, fear, control, lust, fornication, soul ties, etc., but we need to get to that place of surrender. While we can see them in others, we first must question if it's in our own lives. Remember the beam in our own eye... **(Matthew 7:3-5, KJV)**

Also, while going through all of these, it taught me to stay in the fight through finding out who I am in Christ, who He is in me, and what I possess that the enemy did not want me to know that's inside of me. I didn't know back then what I know now. I knew a few basics, but I did not have the spiritual tools that I have now to fight with. However, two is always better than one. It's a blessing when both spouses are on the same page when it comes to fighting the enemy. It's a matter of someone being on guard at all times; when one is attacked, the other should be standing in the gap, if not both. Another thing this has taught me was that the true Love of Christ, the love I have for Jesus, has caused me to love my husband that much more.

I really can't explain how you can love someone more than you did before you got married, before all of the chaos, betrayal, rejection, misunderstandings, etc. It didn't make any sense to me in my natural mind, but in my spirit man, it made a lot of sense! It feels like all the love inside of me was bottled up and reserved for my husband because there was a time it wasn't received. Now it's ready to burst out!

I now understand the meaning of the saying, when a man loves Jesus, he should love you in return. I don't mean love Jesus in word only; I mean love Him indeed!

The breakthrough finally arrived because I trusted my Father! To see what He has done for my family and me right before my eyes, the way that He opened the doors for His Promise to come forth, has me in awe! Remember the vision I shared in the previous chapters, where my son sang by the piano while my husband was standing in the pulpit? God showed me this a few years back, right after I fasted for three days with no food and water. Well, it came to pass, and I sat there in amazement, but not because I didn't believe it. There wasn't a doubt in my mind that God would not do what He said, and there is no way I can move forward ever doubting Him! As I said before, God took me through the process up until this point; I will never forget the work He started in me. Talk about a spiritual boot camp! This was the only way for me to build up my spiritual muscles.

I saw what the enemy was trying to do for a long time, but I also saw what God was showing me as well, so I continued to stay focused on God. My husband and I are still a work in progress. While we are in ***our*** process of reconciliation, God is working on us as individuals and as a couple. I am learning that when your marriage is healthy, your ministry is healthy, and we do better **together** than apart. So, by God's Grace and Mercy, He continues to help us work on our journey of representing Christ the right way.

When I look back over my life and how I first felt the Holy Spirit tugging at my heart to join my "Safe Haven," I never would have imagined God's divine purpose for sending me there. God has a purpose and a plan mapped out for us all, and I am still learning to yield to His ways more and more every day.

Prayerfully, my brother or sister, you will learn to do the same.

I would like to take this moment to write out a prayer...

"First, I want to say thank you, Jesus, for loving me and keeping me. I know that there will be many more things to face as time goes on. I pray for more faith in you to press

toward the mark for the prize of the high calling of God in Christ Jesus." ***(Philippians 3:14, KJV)***

I pray for all marriages.

Lord, I pray that you will give husbands and wives the strength to endure until the end. I pray that they will each find their place in You first and then in their covenant marriages. I pray for peace and understanding. Let no weapon that is formed against them prosper, and every tongue that shall rise against them in judgment, thou shalt condemn. Let this be the servant's heritage of the Lord; their righteousness is of You, saith the Lord.

I pray that you will bless each married couple, those who want to be married, and those on the verge of giving up. Let them understand that all things are working for their good because they love you and are called according to Your Purpose. Let them not pursue their own purpose and agenda, but please give them a desire for your will and plan. I pray that divine knowledge and understanding be given to every individual and married couple concerning what you desire: which is a Kingdom marriage that reveals, promotes, and advances your Kingdom.

Lord God, allow them to grasp that if they surrender their purpose for Your Purpose, their marriage will be truly one, just as you and your son Jesus Christ are one. Help them to decrease so that You may increase them. If any of your children are going through something, help them understand that the cost of standing for YOUR PURPOSE will be worth staying in their ORDAINED COVENANT MARRIAGE and life.

Help them to give it one more day and one more try. Father, help them to keep going so they will finally see the breakthrough you have for them arrive. You are no respecter of persons; if you did it for me, you will do it for them! In Jesus' name, I pray, Amen.

God bless you my brother or sister!

I pray that what I have written has blessed you. Thank you for taking the time to read the second half of my testimony. Although there are many things I didn't share, I pray what you did receive was edifying to your spirit. I also pray that through my life, you are able to see with God, all things are possible. He heals, He restores, and He redeems!

Yours in Christ,

Yavon Smith

About the Author

Yavon Smith obtained a degree in Theology and is currently studying to receive her bachelor's degree in Christian Counseling. She is partnered with an organization called, "Rise Above Defeat."

Yavon serves as a Christian Life Coach and operates as a Deliverance Minister, whose primary focus is helping others tear down spiritual strongholds in their life through the power of the Holy Spirit.

She stands on the scripture in 1 John 5:4, which speaks on the truth that believers can overcome their struggles with the past, habits, and addictions because "everyone born of God overcomes the world."

Yavon is truly passionate about nurturing the youth, imparting into young adults and the elderly to evoke transformative change. Most importantly, she seeks to serve God in whatever capacity He desires her to so that His name can be magnified and glorified.

Contact

To reach Yavon for booking, coaching services, or to share how her story has blessed you, please send an email to: authoryavonsmith@hotmail.com

Are you on social media? Connect with her on Instagram @authoryavonsmith and find her on Facebook at Author Yavon Smith.

www.ingramcontent.com/pod-product-compliance
Lightning Source LLC
LaVergne TN
LVHW020637100826
845148LV00012B/2213

* 9 7 8 0 5 7 8 3 5 6 6 2 4 *